W9-BRT-336

Black Hills

FAMILY FUN GUIDE

2ND Edition

Kindra Gordon

ADVENTURE PUBLICATIONS
CAMBRIDGE, MINNESOTA

DEDICATION

To my husband Bruce, whom I thank for helping me pursue my dreams.

Cover and book design by Jonathan Norberg

Photo credits by page number:

Cover photos: Kindra Gordon: Storybook Island (front, bottom left), Black Elk Peak (front, bottom center), Horseback ride (front, bottom right), Crazy Horse Memorial (back, upper left), President Statue (back, middle right), and Reptile Gardens (back, lower right) **Shutterstock:** Mount Rushmore (front, main)

Beautiful Rushmore Cave, Keystone, SD: 62 (upper left) **Black Hills Central Railroad:** 85 **City of Deadwood and the Deadwood Historic Preservation Commission:** 19 **Kindra Gordon:** 8 (all), 9, 12, 15, 16, 17, 26, 30, 37, 39, 40 (upper left & right), 44, 45, 66, 68, 71, 73, 78, 80, 84 (bottom center), 89, 100 (bottom center), 106, 111, 129, 136 **Maysa Hackens @ How Eye See It Photography:** 98, 112 (bottom center), 118 **High Plains Western Heritage Center:** 48 (upper right) **Historic Homestake Opera House:** 112 (upper left) **Homestake Visitor Center:** 40 **Paul Horsted:** 48 (upper left) **Mary Laflin:** 112 (upper right) **Brian Madetzke/Custer State Park:** 28 **The Mammoth Site of Hot Springs, SD:** 32 (upper right) **Colleen Marsh Olson:** 113 **Kathi Maxson:** 60 **Randee Peterson:** 48 (bottom center) **Sage Studios:** 119 **Sioux Pottery:** 41 **South Dakota Tourism:** 20, 22 (all), 23, 29, 32 (upper left & bottom center), 33, 49, 53, 57, 62 (upper right & bottom center), 63, 84 (upper left & right), 88, 94, 99, 100 (upper right), 101, 108, 117 **Wall Drug Store, Inc.:** 100 (upper left), 104

First Edition 2007
Second Edition 2017
Copyright 2017 by Kindra Gordon
Published by Adventure Publications
An imprint of AdventureKEEN
820 Cleveland Street South
Cambridge, Minnesota 55008
(800) 678-7006
www.adventurepublications.net
All rights reserved
Printed in U.S.A.
ISBN: 978-1-59193-139-3

INTRODUCTION

Wide open spaces, scenic vistas, gurgling streams—it's the stuff that dreams and cherished memories are made of, and you'll find it all in the Black Hills and Badlands of South Dakota.

Best known for the presidential faces of Mount Rushmore, this region often surprises visitors with its natural beauty, tranquil scenery and abundance of interesting places to explore. There's the monumental sculpture at Crazy Horse, and the natural grandeur of Devils Tower, Bear Butte, Spearfish Canyon, Custer State Park and the Badlands. You'll find one-of-a-kind museums, dinosaur displays and Broadway-style theaters. Add to this the excitement of tales of the Old West and narratives from American Indian culture, and you've got more to experience than you can fit in just one family vacation!

The Black Hills offer adventure, history, family fun and even quiet solitude. It's a place people visit over and over again—for the granite spires, the black forest and the pleasant South Dakota pace. For families, it's a memorable destination that often becomes tradition from one generation to the next.

The *Black Hills Family Fun Guide* will complement your adventures and exploration of South Dakota's Black Hills and Badlands. Arranged by theme, this easy-to-read, fact-filled guide describes over 150 attractions—places to go and things to do—in this fascinating region. If you want to pose for an old-time photo, explore a gold mine, take a trail ride, or learn about the area's many patriotic places, this book provides the details of what's offered and where to go. Interspersed within the informative text are history, trivia and interesting tidbits to make your experience in the Black Hills meaningful. At the back of the book (page 130), you will find an index alphabetically arranged by city. So go ahead and explore, and most importantly, enjoy this fascinating region!

While exploring the Black Hills, visitors are encouraged to use caution and keep safety top of mind. Many outdoor areas are rugged, remote terrain and are home to rattlesnakes and mountain lions. Within Custer State Park, visitors are also reminded to keep a safe distance from the buffalo. Additionally, the Black Hills can experience extreme heat in summer and below zero wind chills in winter. Visitors should dress appropriately for the season and always have drinking water available.

Table of Contents

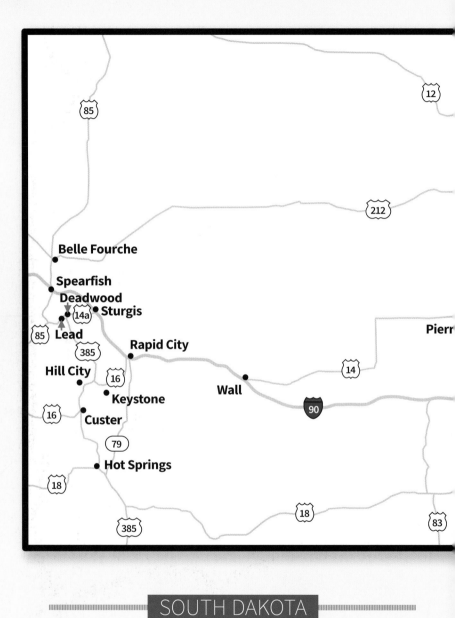

SOUTH DAKOTA

Sioux Falls

CHAPTER 1

Famous Faces to Visit

Throughout the Black Hills are monumental tributes to famous people from the past. Of course, the titanic faces of Washington, Jefferson, Roosevelt and Lincoln carved in stone at Mount Rushmore are the most well-known memorial in this region, but there are many other Black Hills attractions that honor historical figures and share the stories of their lives. You'll find several sights with a presidential theme, as well as memorials to American Indian leaders and Wild West legends.

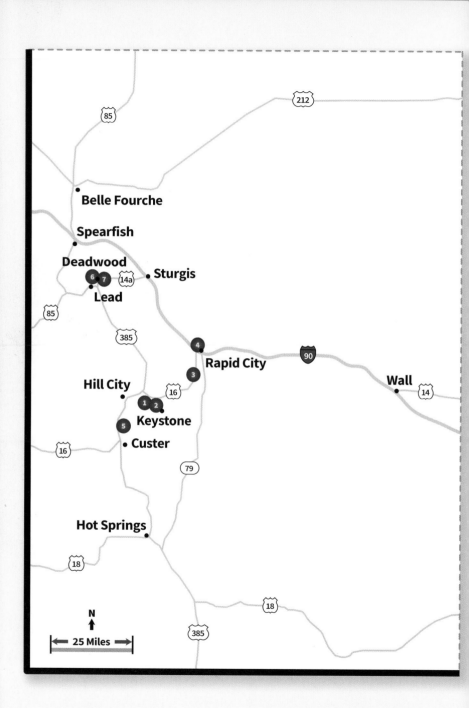

Presidential Places

Historical Figures

Presidential Places

1 MOUNT RUSHMORE NATIONAL MEMORIAL

Carved from a mountain that stands more than a mile high, a visit to Mount Rushmore instills visitors young and old with a stirring sense of American pride. Created by sculptor Gutzon Borglum as a tribute to American ideals, the four Presidents—George Washington, Thomas Jefferson, Theodore Roosevelt and Abraham Lincoln—were chosen to be part of the monument because they symbolized the birth, growth, preservation and development of the United States.

South Dakota's signature attraction is the presidential faces on Mount Rushmore

In August 1927, Borglum began drilling on the mountain, at the age of 60. After Borglum's death in 1941, his son Lincoln completed the project on October 31, 1941. It took a span of 14 years and cost nearly 1 million dollars ($989,992.32, to be exact) to carve the four faces, with $836,000 of that cost paid by the federal government.

Today, over 2 million people visit Mount Rushmore each year. Once you've admired the faces on the mountain, take time to explore and enjoy the grounds surrounding this symbol of our nation's democracy.

Fun activities include finding your home state's flag among the colorful **Avenue of Flags** that greets visitors as they enter Mount Rushmore. The promenade of flags leads to the **Grandview Terrace** for a majestic view of the four faces. Then, hike the paved **Presidential Trail** to get a close-up view of the granite sculpture. The trail makes a half-mile loop and includes 422 stairs; however, the first quarter mile of the path is wheelchair accessible and leads to the base of the monument. Mountain goats can often be glimpsed cavorting in the rocks around Rushmore.

To learn more about the monument, watch the brief film at the **Lincoln Borglum Visitor Center**, which explains how and why the monument was created. Then, view the historical exhibits on display in the museum, including a mock dynamite blast for kids. Also plan to visit the **Sculptor's Studio** where Gutzon Borglum's original model and many of the tools used to carve the mountain are still kept.

A **Junior Ranger Program**, offered for children aged 5 to 12, explains how Mount Rushmore was constructed and teaches them about the National Park Service. For children aged 13 and older—and adults—several **Ranger Programs** are offered that help visitors understand and appreciate national parks, with a special emphasis on Mount Rushmore. Audio wands are available for rent to hear the story of Mount Rushmore through music, narration, interviews, historic recordings and sound effects while you walk on a scenic route around the park. Ask about the programs at the Visitor Information Center near the entrance or call (605) 574-3165 for more information.

The **Evening Lighting Ceremony** is a popular Mount Rushmore event as well. The patriotic program in the outdoor amphitheatre includes a short film about the monument and concludes as floodlights reveal the presidents' faces lit up against the night sky. The program is held at 9 p.m. nightly from late May through mid-August. During the latter portion of August through September, the program begins at 8 p.m. From October through mid-May, the sculpture is illuminated at dusk, but there is no program. If you visit, dress warm for the evening ceremony, as night temperatures are chilly in the mountains.

During your visit, be sure to drive around Mount Rushmore on SD Hwy. 244 for a unique profile view of George Washington.

A bookstore, gift shop, restaurant and snack shop are also available on site at Mount Rushmore National Memorial.

Open year-round; Admission free, but fee charged for parking; 13000 SD Hwy. 244, Bldg. 31, Ste. 1, Keystone, SD 57751; (605) 574-2523; www.nps.gov/moru

Western heroes, such as Buffalo Bill Cody, Lewis and Clark and American Indian leader Red Cloud, were first considered for the monument.

Jefferson's face was originally on the left side of Washington's (as you look at the sculpture); it was moved to the right because of flaws in the rock.

② NATIONAL PRESIDENTIAL WAX MUSEUM

Meet each of America's presidents as you walk through this unique museum. On display are realistic, life-size wax figures of every U.S. president, each in period costumes and historical settings, such as John F. Kennedy in the Oval Office with John, Jr. playing beneath the desk, and Nixon aboard the *USS Hornet* welcoming the Apollo 11 astronauts home from their moon flight. President Clinton's red, white and blue saxophone and Florida's controversial ballot boxes are among other intriguing exhibits. All of the U.S. presidents are on display, and in total there are 100 wax figures of people, many of whom had an important role in American history.

Open April through October; Admission charged; 609 US Hwy. 16A, Keystone, SD 57751; (605) 666-4455; www.presidentialwaxmuseum.com

Past presidents have found the Black Hills a favorite place to visit. In 1927, President Calvin Coolidge spent the summer at Custer Park's State Game Lodge and Resort, leading it to be nicknamed the "Summer White House." The resort was a favorite place of President Eisenhower, too. For more about Custer State Park, see Chapter 6, page 67.

③ AMERICA'S FOUNDING FATHERS EXHIBIT

At this interactive exhibit visitors can witness one of the most historic events in U.S. history: the drafting and eventual signing of the Declaration of Independence. Housed within a brick building that is a near-replica of Philadelphia's historic Independence Hall, once inside, visitors will find themselves in a setting reminiscent of 1776, when the first draft of the Declaration of Independence was presented to the Second Continental Congress.

The three-dimensional, life-size exhibit is a sculptural rendition of John Trumbull's historic painting, "The Declaration of Independence," which depicts more than 40 patriots in Independence Hall. While Trumbull's painting is considered to be an imagined scene, this provides an opportunity for visitors to also imagine what America's founding fathers experienced as they forged ahead with declaring independence from England. A 20-minute audio presentation shares insights from several of the depicted individuals, including Thomas Jefferson, John Adams and Benjamin Franklin. Adding to the experience, visitors have a chance to add their own name to the Declaration of Independence.

Travel back to 1776 with a trip to this near-replica of Independence Hall

An outdoor shooting range is also on site; there, visitors can shoot the Kentucky long rifle, one of the weapons used during the Revolutionary War. Participants receive a brief history on the weapon, along with instruction on loading and firing, and get to shoot it three times. Shooters must sign a liability release and be at least 16 years of age to participate.

Open May through September; Admission charged; rifle shooting requires an additional fee; 9815 US Hwy. 16, Rapid City, SD 57702; (605) 877-6043; http://foundingfathersblackhills.com

4 CITY OF PRESIDENTS PROJECT

Throughout downtown Rapid City, life-size bronze statues of past U.S. presidents adorn the street corners. Each presidential sculpture is a near replica of that individual with the actual height and dress matching the period in which they lived—Ronald Reagan and Theodore Roosevelt wearing cowboy hats, Dwight Eisenhower in military uniform, Andrew Jackson in a flowing cape, and John Adams in a waistcoat and vest. The project began in 2000, and today all past presidents are on display, with plans to add each successive president. An online interactive walking guide provides the location and more information about each president and can be accessed through the website below.

Accessible year-round; Free admission; Information Center open June through September; 631 Main St., Rapid City, SD 57701; (800) 487-3223; www.visitrapidcity.com/things-to-do/city-presidents

NEAT TO KNOW

Look for the two American Indian themed sculptures—titled *Iye Na Oyate Ki* and *Mitakuye Oyasin*—on display along Rapid City's Main Street.

Passage of Wind and Water is the theme of sculpture carvings on the large granite spires that surround Main Street Square in downtown Rapid City.

Art Alley, between Rapid City's 6th and 7th Streets, is a constantly changing display of colorful murals and pop art. It's a tribute to freedom of expression.

Tip your cap (or top hat) to James Monroe at the City of Presidents Project

Historical Figures

5 CRAZY HORSE MEMORIAL

This mountain sculpture of Lakota leader Chief Crazy Horse is being constructed as a tribute to the North American Indians. Korczak Ziolkowski began carving Crazy Horse in 1948 at the request of Indian leaders who wanted to create a memorial that would complement Mount Rushmore and remind the world that "American Indians have great heroes, too." Interestingly, Ziolkowski worked on Mount Rushmore for a short time in 1939 with its creator, Gutzon Borglum.

A work in progress, the Crazy Horse Memorial is a fantastic stop

Despite Ziolkowski's death in 1982, his wife Ruth and seven of their ten children continued to work on the sculpture, which is a nonprofit project financed from private funds. In 1998, 50 years after the project was started, the 9-story-high face of Crazy Horse was completed. Ruth died in 2014, but the Ziolkowski children are continuing to carry on the dream of their parents. Blocking out the 22-story-high horse's head is currently in progress, and upon completion (which hinges on weather and financing), the figure of the chief astride his pony will be 563 feet high and 641 feet long, the largest statue in the world.

Although visitors can get a good view of the Crazy Horse mountain monument from US Hwy. 385, the on-site **Welcome Center** provides an educational overview about the creation of the monument and American Indian culture. The informative film *Dynamite and Dreams* in the visitor center profiles Ziolkowski's vision for Crazy Horse Memorial and the surrounding campus. On-site displays include scale models of the statue and exhibits explaining the drilling and blasting process. Also on site, the **Indian Museum of North America** features an extensive display of Indian artifacts such as beaded moccasins and an authentic teepee. The studio-home and workshop of Ziolkowski showcases sculptures he created through his lifetime. A bookstore, gift shop, restaurant and cultural center where authentic American Indian jewelry and art are offered for sale are all located within the complex.

For a nominal fee, rustic bus rides are offered to the base of the mountain for close-up viewing. Van rides to the top of the mountain are also offered for a larger fee and require a reservation. Call (605) 673-4681.

Blasting on the mountain occurs intermittently through the summer with a ceremonial blast held each October on Native American Day. The monument is lit nightly at dusk for one hour. From Memorial Day weekend through October 1, a laser light show is held nightly (times vary and a schedule is listed on their website). The show features colorful animations, still photography, sound effects and laser beams choreographed to music.

Open year-round; Admission charged; 12151 Avenue of the Chiefs (5 miles from Custer), Crazy Horse, SD 57730; (605) 673-4681; https://crazyhorsememorial.org

NEAT TO KNOW

For visitors who like to hike, an annual volksmarch is held the first full weekend in June and gives the public a once-a-year chance to hike up the mountain to stand in front of the 9-story-high face of Crazy Horse. Round-trip, the hike is 6.2 miles. A fall volksmarch is held on a Sunday in late September or early October in conjunction with Custer State Park's Buffalo Roundup weekend events.

Ironically, Crazy Horse was chosen as the subject for the mountain sculpture, even though there is no documented photo of him. It is said that he refused to ever have his photo taken, and asked photographers, "Would you imprison my shadow, too?" Thus, the sculpture of him is not a literal likeness, but rather a tribute to the spirit of the man and is based on detailed descriptions of Crazy Horse.

6 MOUNT MORIAH CEMETERY

This hillside cemetery is the final resting place for many of the Old West's legendary characters. Most notable is James Butler "Wild Bill" Hickok, who was shot in Deadwood during a poker game on August 2, 1876. A bronze monument marks his gravesite. Calamity Jane, who was born as Martha Canary and claimed to be Wild Bill's sweetheart, is buried beside him. Visitors to the cemetery will also see graves of Potato Creek Johnny, Preacher Smith, Seth Bullock—Deadwood's first sheriff—and others with historical ties to Deadwood. From Mount Moriah, visitors also get a bird's-eye view of Deadwood in the gulch below.

Open year-round; Admission charged; 10 Mt. Moriah Rd., Deadwood, SD 57732; (605) 722-0837; www.cityofdeadwood.com/ (select Mount Moriah Cemetery from the menu)

Wild Bill Hickok's tombstone, which misspells his name

NEAT TO KNOW

To learn more about Deadwood's past, consider taking a narrated bus tour outlining the town's history and its colorful residents. Three companies offer similar one-hour bus tours that wind through Deadwood and stop at Mount Moriah. Tours are offered several times daily from May to October with pick-up points along Deadwood's Main Street. Tour companies include:

Original Deadwood Tours: (605) 578-2091 or www.deadwoodtour.com

Alkali Ike Tours: (605) 578-3147 or www.alkaliiketours.com

Boot Hill Tours: (605) 580-5231 or http://boothilltours.com

A great way to see Deadwood is to jump aboard the green trolleys that meander through town. The trolleys run at regular intervals between all hotels and other key stops in Deadwood. Trolleys run year-round and only cost $1 per person.

Old West history also comes to the life with the **Main Street Shootouts**, a historical reenactment of a Western shootout presented at 2, 4 and 6 p.m. daily along Deadwood's Main Street. Additionally, a reenactment of the Shooting of Wild Bill is held daily inside Saloon No. 10 at 1, 3, 5, and 7 p.m. The free performances are given from Memorial Day through early September. For more information, call (800) 344-8826 or visit www.deadwoodalive.com.

7 TRIAL OF JACK MCCALL

Get a glimpse of the many characters who roamed Deadwood during the Gold Rush Days. This family-friendly show recreates the actual trial that took place in Deadwood after Jack McCall murdered Wild Bill Hickok. As the story goes, McCall shot the unsuspecting Wild Bill while he was engrossed in a game of poker at Saloon No. 10. Hickok's final hand was a pair of aces and eights, which ever since has been known as "the dead man's hand."

Enjoy the re-enactment of a Western shootout on Deadwood's Main Street

The reenactment, which is held Monday through Saturday, begins at 7:35 p.m. outside Saloon No. 10 on Main Street with the shooting of Hickok and the capture of McCall. Afterward, the trial gets underway in the Historic Masonic Temple Theatre (next to the Silverado) at 8 p.m. The performance is historically accurate with a large dose of entertainment provided by audience members participating as jurors.

Performed Memorial Day through Labor Day; Admission charged; PO Box 190, Deadwood, SD 57732; (800) 344-8826; www.deadwoodalive.com/trial-of-jack-mccall

NEAT TO KNOW: DEADWOOD HISTORY

Saloon No. 10 in Deadwood bills itself as a museum, with antiques and oddities spread throughout the historic bar, including the chair in which Wild Bill Hickok reportedly died. Families are welcome to view this historic selection at 657 Main Street until 8 p.m. For more information, call (800) 952-9398 or visit www.saloon10. com. The original 1876 location of Saloon No. 10, previously called Nuttal & Mann's Saloon, was actually across the street at 622 Main Street. When a fire claimed many of the buildings along that block in 1879, the bar moved up the street.

To this day, some say Seth Bullock haunts the **Bullock Hotel**, which he established in 1896 on Deadwood's Main Street. Ghost tours can be scheduled for a nominal fee; tours last 45 minutes. For more information or for hotel reservations, call the **Bullock** at (800) 336-1876 or visit www.historicbullock.com. Deadwood's Historic Fairmont Hotel, located at 628 Main Street, is also rumored to be haunted and has been featured on TV shows including *Ghost Adventures* and *The Dead Files.* Paranormal tours can be scheduled by calling (605) 578-2205.

Two famous women associated with Deadwood's Gold Rush lived in nearby Sturgis. **Annie Tallent**, the first white woman to come to the Black Hills in 1874, came to the area in search of gold and became one of the region's first schoolteachers. Her home at 1603 West Main Street is now a private residence. **Poker Alice**, a cigar-smoking cardsharp who owned the rowdiest honky-tonk in the state, also lived in Sturgis. Her home still stands at 1802 Junction Avenue. Poker Alice is buried in St. Aloysius Catholic Cemetery, which is directly across from the Annie Tallent house.

CHAPTER 2

Buffalo, Bears and Reptiles, Oh My!

The Black Hills does not have a traditional zoo, per se, but it does offer many attractions with live animals on display, including everything from area wildlife, such as bison, to exotic reptiles and friendly farm pets. Options range from park-like settings where you can see animals up close to scenic drives through the region's state and national parks where wild animals roam free.

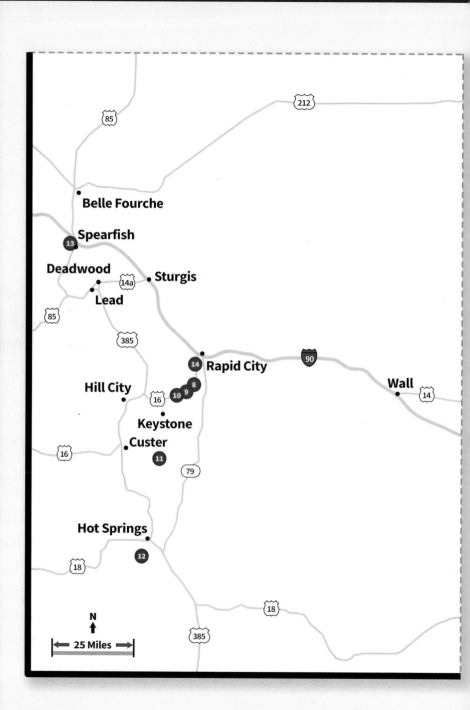

Belle Fourche

Spearfish **13**

Deadwood

Lead **14a** Sturgis

85

385

14 Rapid City

90

Wall **14**

Hill City

16 **10** **9** **8**

Keystone

Custer

16

11

79

Hot Springs

18

12

18

N

25 Miles

385

Animal Adventures

Fish Fun

Animal Adventures

8 REPTILE GARDENS

It goes without saying that most kids will love this place—snakes, Komodo dragons, alligators, crocodiles and lizards are all here. But the rest of the family will equally be captivated by the many activities that Reptile Gardens has to offer.

Open since the Great Depression, Reptile Gardens is a must-see

Operating since 1937, Reptile Gardens is well known for its extensive collection of reptiles, fossils, and its two (literally) big attractions: Maniac, a 1,200-pound crocodile, and the giant tortoises here that are over 100 years old. The Sky Dome is a jungle-like setting with free-flying birds and nonvenomous snakes amid tropical orchids and colorful, lush botanical plants. Three educational shows (Birds of Prey, Alligators and Crocodiles, and Snakes) are informative and entertaining. They are presented several times daily during the summer months and will be a highlight of your visit. Bewitched Village is an Old West town perfect for exploring or posing for silly photos. Allow time to stroll the flower-filled grounds, visit the prairie dog exhibit, which includes an underground tunnel for kids and adults, and browse the reptile-themed gift shop.

Open March through November; Admission charged; 8955 US Hwy. 16 (6 miles south of Rapid City on US Hwy. 16); Rapid City, SD 57702; (605) 342-5873 or (800) 335-0275; www.reptilegardens.com

9 BEAR COUNTRY USA

Visitors are guaranteed to see wildlife in this three-mile drive-through park. It is home to 20 species of North American mammals, including black bears and grizzlies, along with Arctic wolves, bighorn sheep, reindeer, elk, Rocky Mountain goats and mountain lions. Opened in 1972, today the family-run entity has the largest collection of privately owned black bears in the world. As you drive your own personal vehicle through the park, it's fun to keep your eyes peeled for whatever animal may be lounging nearby. For safety, it's imperative to keep all vehicle windows rolled up and doors closed. At the end of the drive-through portion of the park, there is a snack bar and picnic area, as well as a walking path past fenced exhibits featuring smaller wildlife, including bear cubs, wolf pups and other young animals born in the spring, giving visitors the opportunity to enjoy a closer look at the animals. The on-site Bear's Den gift shop and gallery cater to wildlife enthusiasts.

Open mid-April through November; Admission charged; 13820 US Hwy. 16 (8 miles south of Rapid City), Rapid City, SD 57702; (605) 343-2290; www.bearcountryusa.com

10 OLD MACDONALD'S PETTING FARM

Kids can get up close and personal with dozens of friendly farm animals at this petting zoo. Activities include feeding fish, ducks and geese in their ponds, petting goats and calves, as well as riding on ponies and a kid-sized tractor train. In the poultry house, you can even watch chicks hatch from their eggs. The whole family will have a squeal at the pig races (held various times throughout the day), and it's always entertaining to watch the goats trip-tropping over their very own bridge. There is a snack bar and gift shop on site, or you can pack a picnic and enjoy it at the play area. Guided tours, school field trips and special rates for birthday parties are available.

Open May through mid-September, some weekends through October; Admission charged; 23691 Busted Five Court (9 miles south of Rapid City on US Hwy. 16), Rapid City, SD 57702; (605) 737-4815; www.oldmacdonaldsfarmrc.com

11 CUSTER STATE PARK

At 70,000-plus acres, Custer State Park is truly the place where "buffalo roam and the deer and the antelope play." This well-known park is just south of Mount Rushmore and ranks as the nation's second-largest state park. It is home to nearly 1,300 buffalo, along with elk, deer, bighorn sheep, prairie dogs, and the "begging" burros (that aren't shy about approaching cars and begging for food).

Within the park, the 18-mile **Wildlife Loop** is a popular drive known for providing breathtaking views of the park's many animals. Several other scenic drives also wind through the park, offering picture-perfect vantage points of the park's forests, grassy valleys and abundant wildlife. **Needles Highway, Iron Mountain Road, Horse Thief Lake Road** and **Sylvan Lake Road** make up the 70-mile Peter Norbeck Scenic Byway, which has been named one of America's 10 Most Outstanding Byways.

Of course, you can do more than drive through the park. The **Custer State Park Visitor Center** (located at the junction of the Wildlife Loop Road and US Hwy.

16A) features a large interactive map, 20-foot-tall scale models of the Cathedral Spires and a 100-seat theater where a park film, narrated by actor Kevin Costner, introduces visitors to the many different aspects of the park. Additionally, the **Peter Norbeck Visitor Center** on US Hwy. 16A and the **Wildlife Station Visitor Center** on the Wildlife Loop both provide more information about the park. Available activities include hiking, mountain biking, rock climbing, swimming, canoeing, paddle boating and trail rides. Visitors are also welcome to snowshoe or cross-country ski in the winter. The visitor centers can provide maps for trails in the park and information about the park's Junior Naturalist and Ranger Programs, which allow visitors to explore the outdoors and learn more about the Black Hills and Custer State Park.

Open year-round; Admission charged; 13329 US Hwy. 16A, Custer, SD 57730; (605) 255-4515; www.custerstatepark.info

FOR MORE ACTIVITIES AVAILABLE IN CUSTER STATE PARK:

Chapter 6: Custer State Park, page 67

NEAT TO KNOW : BEVY OF BUFFALO

Known for its large herd of buffalo, Custer State Park offers two unique opportunities to marvel at these shaggy beasts. Through the summer, **Buffalo Safari Jeep Rides** leave from the State Game Lodge and Resort in the park and allow visitors to get into the backcountry to see the buffalo roam. In the fall, Custer State Park conducts an annual **Buffalo Roundup**, which allows visitors to watch as the thundering herd of buffalo is moved into corrals where some animals will be sorted and sold in order to keep the herd a manageable size. For more information, call (605) 255-4541 or visit http://custerresorts.com/activities/.

Buffalo are always exciting to see in Custer State Park

12 BLACK HILLS WILD HORSE SANCTUARY

Over 500 wild horses run free in the open prairie of this sanctuary and working ranch, which was established by author and conservationist Dayton Hyde for wild mustangs rescued from the oversized herds found on government lands in the West. Two- or three-hour guided tours are offered several times daily and showcase these magnificent mustangs in the wilderness along the Cheyenne River, which they now call home. Petroglyphs, teepee rings and abundant wildlife sightings add to the experience. Cabin accommodations are available for guests interested in an overnight experience.

Open year-round; Admission charged; 12163 Highland Rd. (13 miles southwest of Hot Springs on SD Hwy. 71), PO Box 998, Hot Springs, SD 57747; (605) 745-5955; www.wildmustangs.com

Wild mustangs roam free along the Cheyenne River wilderness south of Hot Springs

NEAT TO KNOW

On your way to or from the sanctuary, plan a picnic stop at Keith Park or Cascade Falls, also found along SD Hwy. 71. Both spots offer scenic settings with natural flowing springs, picnic tables and restrooms. The cool waters of Cascade Falls are also considered one of South Dakota's best natural swimming holes. Check out www.fs.fed.us/wildflowers/regions/Rocky_Mountain/CascadeSprings/ for more details.

Fish Fun

13 D.C. BOOTH HISTORIC NATIONAL FISH HATCHERY

Established by the U.S. government in 1896, this hatchery played an instrumental role in introducing trout into the Black Hills and Yellowstone National Park. Today, the facility remains an active hatchery, with 20,000 to 30,000 rainbow and brown trout from the site stocked each year into nearby lakes and streams for anglers to enjoy. At the hatchery, large underwater viewing windows provide visitors a fun nose-to-nose view of the fish. Visitors can also purchase pellets to feed the fish in the raceways or from the bridge.

Check out the fish through the underwater viewing windows

Set on 10 picturesque acres along Spearfish Creek and adjacent to the Spearfish City Park, the D.C. Booth hatchery grounds feature several unique buildings, including the elegant Booth House fitted with Victorian furnishings and the Von Bayer Museum of Fish Culture, which collects and preserves hatchery artifacts from throughout the country. The site even has a restored fisheries railcar. Two hiking trails provide a scenic overlook of the grounds. The entire hatchery site is listed on the National Register of Historic Places.

The Pond Gift Shop offers fish food, nature and history books, toys, gifts and hatchery souvenirs.

Grounds open year-round, buildings open May through September; Free admission; 423 Hatchery Circle, Spearfish, SD 57783; (605) 642-7730; http://dcboothfishhatchery.org

14 CLEGHORN SPRINGS STATE FISH HATCHERY

This working hatchery raises and releases over 500,000 rainbow trout and salmon annually, primarily to stock South Dakota's lakes and rivers. It's a popular place for field trips or family outings, and the hatchery provides food for visitors to feed to the fish. The hatchery's Aquatic Education Interpretive Center provides informative displays about fish hatchery operations, fly-fishing and stream rehabilitation efforts. From September through May the hatchery accommodates scheduled tours, which are available Monday through Friday.

Grounds open year-round, visitor center open May through mid-August; Free admission; 4725 Jackson Blvd., Rapid City, SD 57702; (605) 394-4100; http://gfp.sd.gov/fishing-boating/hatcheries/cleghorn-hatchery.aspx

FOR MORE WILDLIFE SIGHTINGS, SEE ALSO:

Chapter 3: Badlands National Park, Wall, page 36

Chapter 6: Wind Cave National Park, Hot Springs, page 78

Dinosaurs Galore

Thousands of dinosaur fossils have been uncovered across South Dakota, including Sue, the largest and most complete *Tyrannosaurus rex* ever found. It was unearthed in 1990, near Faith, South Dakota, and is now on display in Chicago at The Field Museum. While Sue is no longer here, South Dakota's Black Hills still offer a variety of places where visitors can examine dinosaur bones and other prehistoric fossils and learn about the gigantic creatures that roamed the earth millions of years ago. Rapid City's one-of-a-kind Dinosaur Park is also popular, thanks to its large sculptures of these prehistoric beasts.

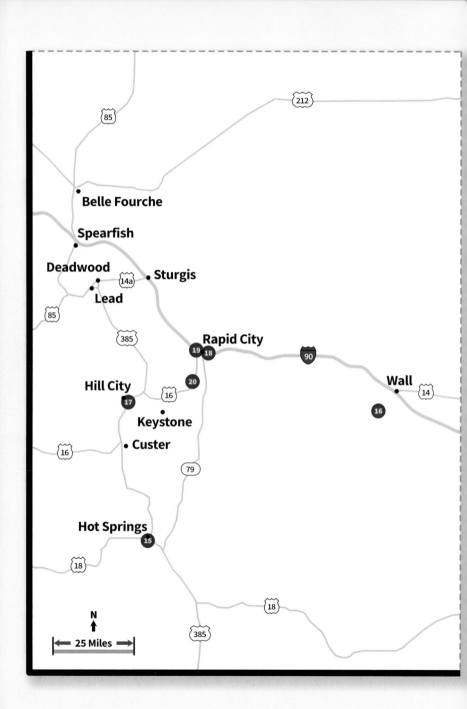

Belle Fourche

Spearfish

Deadwood

Sturgis

Lead

Rapid City

Hill City

Keystone

Custer

Wall

Hot Springs

N

25 Miles

Fascinating Fossils

Dinosaur Delights

Fascinating Fossils

15 MAMMOTH SITE

The Black Hills' best-known fossil find is likely the Mammoth Site, which is an amazing prehistoric sinkhole where the fossils of over 100 mammoths (relatives of the elephant) and other early creatures were perfectly preserved during the last Ice Age. The fossils, which are estimated to be about 26,000 years old, weren't discovered until 1974 when a bulldozer working on a housing project unearthed a mammoth tusk. The housing project was stopped and an enclosed research facility was eventually built over the fossilized sinkhole.

Today, visitors can take guided tours to view the actual excavation in progress. Walkways constructed over the site allow visitors to see the fossils as they are painstakingly unearthed. Active digs are only conducted in July, but tours of the site, which show various stages of the excavation process, are given year-round. More than 60 Columbian and woolly mammoths and other creatures from the Pleistocene era have already been excavated, but more are still being dug out, making it the world's largest mammoth research facility.

The Ice Age Exhibit Hall adjacent to the excavation area includes displays of life-size mammoth replicas and features a mock dig area that lets kids excavate fiberglass fossil replicas. Youngsters aged 4 to 13 can even take part in the Junior Paleontologist Excavation, a simulated dig held daily from June 1 to August 15. A small fee is charged for the hour-long session. Make reservations for the program online or call (605) 745-6017. Kids will also enjoy roaming the gift shop, which is stocked with prehistoric-themed books, puzzles, games and clothing.

Open year-round; Admission charged; 1800 US Hwy. 18 BYP, PO Box 692, Hot Springs, SD 57747; (605) 745-6017; www.mammothsite.com

16 BADLANDS NATIONAL PARK

Badlands National Park proves that South Dakota wasn't just home to dinosaurs; the state was also home to three-toed horses, saber-toothed cats, and giant rhinoceros-like beasts called titanotheres, all of which roamed the area some 30 million years ago. The **Ben Reifel Visitor Center** and the **Fossil Exhibit Trail** in this national park both offer interpretive displays and fossil replicas that tell the story of these early Badlands creatures. The visitor center includes natural history exhibits, a working laboratory that allows visitors to watch paleontologists at work, a film highlighting the park and a bookstore with a variety of titles about the region. The **Saber Site** is a fossil quarry, located just outside the visitor center. It was established after a seven-year-old girl discovered a fossil in this same spot while participating in a Junior Ranger program. She reported her find to the park ranger, allowing paleontologists to identify the fossil as the skull of an extinct saber-toothed cat, Hoplophoneus. The site is staffed by paleontologists and park rangers through the summer. Additionally, the quarter-mile Fossil

Exhibit Trail is one of the park's most popular attractions and wheelchair accessible. Fossil excavation has also been in progress near the **Conata Basin Picnic Area**. Outdoor exhibits explain some of the area findings, as well as what life was like here during prehistoric times.

While visiting the Badlands, be sure to drive SD Hwy. 240, also known as the **Badlands Loop Road**. The 38-mile scenic drive showcases the park's tinted spires and multicolored rock formations, most of which were created by erosion due to the effects of wind and water. The road has many pullouts for scenic vistas and offers marked hiking trails. Buffalo, pronghorn antelope, bighorn sheep, mule deer and prairie dogs may be seen throughout the park.

There's no place like the Badlands

Cedar Pass Lodge, next door to the Ben Reifel Visitor Center, has a gift shop with pottery, beadwork, jewelry, and traditional souvenirs such as postcards, T-shirts and coffee mugs. During the tourism season (April 15 to October 15), the lodge's restaurant serves Indian tacos, buffalo burgers and other entrees. For lodging within the park, there's a campground, as well as a motel and small cabins for rent near Cedar Pass. Call (605) 433-5460 or (877) 386-4383, or visit www.cedarpasslodge.com for more information.

Summer night sky viewing is offered at the **Cedar Pass Campground Amphitheater** on Friday through Monday nights. Rangers will point out constellations, stars and planets, and telescopes are provided to enjoy the spectacular, light-pollution-free skyscape.

Open year-round; admission charged; 25216 Ben Reifel Rd. (8 miles south of Wall), PO Box 6, Interior, SD 57750; (605) 433-5361; www.nps.gov/badl

NEAT TO KNOW: NEAR THE BADLANDS

The **Prairie Homestead** near the east entrance of the Badlands National Park (I-90 Exit 131) wasn't home to dinosaurs, but it is on the National Register of Historic Places and is the only original sod dwelling on display in South Dakota. Tours of the sod shanty and outbuildings give a sense of what life may have been like on the rugged prairie. A gift shop and snack bar are also operated on site. Open May through mid-October; admission is charged. Call (605) 433-5400 or visit www.prairiehomestead.com.

World-famous **Wall Drug** also offers dinosaur fun. A life-size *Apatosaurus* greets visitors as they enter town near I-90 Exit 110 and offers a place to stop and picnic with a scenic view of the Badlands. At Wall Drug's Back Yard Mall you'll find an animated, roaring *Tyrannosaurus rex* and a smaller cement dinosaur that kids can climb on amid the historical gift shops and other family-friendly displays. Call (605) 279-2175 or visit www.walldrug.com. For more about Wall Drug, see Chapter 8, page 104.

17 BLACK HILLS INSTITUTE OF GEOLOGICAL RESEARCH MUSEUM & EVERYTHING PREHISTORIC GIFT SHOP

Dinosaur devotees will be in awe at the large collection of fossils on display at this museum—and equally impressed by the extensive offering of fossil- and geology-themed collectibles in the adjacent Everything Prehistoric Gift Shop. The authentic fossils of Stan, the largest male *Tyrannosaurus rex* ever found, take center stage in the museum display alongside hundreds of natural history exhibits, including fossils from the Cretaceous period, dinosaur eggs, and mineral and meteorite collections.

Open year-round; Admission charged; 117 Main St., PO Box 643, Hill City, SD 57745; (605) 574-3919; www.bhigr.com

18 MUSEUM OF GEOLOGY

Located on the campus of the South Dakota School of Mines and Technology, this museum collection includes prehistoric mammals, marine reptiles and dinosaurs from the Black Hills and Badlands region, as well as fossils and mineral collections from around the globe. Interpretive paintings hang above the major fossil displays depicting what the animals looked like in prehistoric times. Kids will also enjoy the colorful rock collection—especially the fluorescent room with rocks that glow under a black light.

Open year-round; Free admission; 501 E St. Joseph St,. O'Harra Bldg., Third Fl., Rapid City, SD 57701; (605) 394-2467; www.sdsmt.edu/Academics/Museum-of-Geology/Home/

Dinosaur Delights

19 DINOSAUR PARK

Atop Skyline Drive in the center of Rapid City, this unique park features seven enormous replicas of prehistoric reptiles. The park was built in the 1930s and the super-size dinosaurs can be seen from many points in the city. While little ones clamor around these Jurassic concrete creatures, adults can marvel at the breathtaking view of the city and surrounding area. The adjacent gift shop offers a variety of dinosaur items, including books and toys to T-shirts. Evening lighting gives the statues an eerie glow on the hilltop until 10 p.m.

Open May to October; Free admission; 940 Skyline Dr, Rapid City, SD 57701; (605) 343-8687; www.blackhillsbadlands.com/business/dinosaur-park

Marvel at the dinosaurs and the view of Rapid City at Dinosaur Park

20 DINOSAUR MUSEUM

Here you'll find 50 life-size dinosaur replicas to marvel at, and additional activities for kids to enjoy, including a mirror maze, a movie theater, a fossil dig and mini-golf. A birthday party area and a dinosaur-themed gift shop are also offered.

Open May to September; Admission charged; 8973 US Hwy. 16, Rapid City, SD 57702; (605) 342-8140; www.blackhillsbadlands.com/business/dinosaur-museum

FOR OTHER FOSSILS ON DISPLAYS, SEE ALSO:

Chapter 2: Reptile Gardens, Rapid City, page 26

Chapter 5: Journey Museum, Rapid City, page 52; Adams Museum, Deadwood, page 52; Vore Buffalo Jump, Sundance, WY, page 57

Chapter 8: Petrified Forest of the Black Hills, page 109

CHAPTER 4

See It Made—Or Mined

23 BLACK HILLS MINING MUSEUM

Here, a 50-minute simulated underground tour provides a comprehensive look at the differences between early-day and modern underground mining. Also on display in the museum are historic photographs, artifacts and mining equipment. Visitors to the museum even have a chance to strike the "mother lode" by panning for their own gold.

Open May through October; Admission charged; 323 W Main St., Lead, SD 57754; (605) 584-1605; www.blackhillsminingmuseum.com

The Black Hills Mining Museum showcases the region's mining techniques from yesteryear

24 SANFORD LAB HOMESTAKE VISITOR CENTER

This is the site of one of the oldest and deepest gold mines in the Western Hemisphere, reaching more than 8,000 feet underground. Established in 1876, the Homestake Mine has been called "the richest 100 square miles on Earth"; in operation for more than a century, its underground shafts and open cut produced more than 41 million ounces of gold and 9 million ounces of silver. The mine closed in 2002, and today the 370 miles of underground tunnels provide the perfect facility for the Sanford Underground Laboratory, which houses multiple physics experiments exploring the areas of dark matter and neutrino research.

At the visitor center, a free exhibit features photographs of the mine during its heyday, videos, and mining artifacts highlighting the Homestake Mine and the city of Lead. A 3-D model of the underground mine also provides insight into the mine's interior down to the 8,000-foot level. The outdoor deck offers an amazing view of the previously mined Open Cut, which is a mile wide and over 1,000 feet deep.

To gather more in-depth information, one-hour guided tours are offered from Memorial Day through Labor Day and include a trip through historic Lead, and a surface tour of the Sanford Underground Research Facility. Tours highlight the mining process that once occurred and the science experiments now being conducted. Stops include a visit to the hoist room where more than 5,000 feet of steel rope take personnel to the underground. This unique hoist system has been in operation at the facility since 1939, and on occasion, tour groups will see the hoists in action. Another tour stop is the state-of-the-art Waste Water Treatment Plant that was designed by Homestake Mining Company and is still in use today.

Open year-round; Fee charged for tours; 160 W Main St., Lead, SD 57754; (605) 584-3110; http://sanfordlabhomestake.com

NEAT TO KNOW

Golf enthusiasts might enjoy the chance to get a unique "Hole in One." For a fee, you can hit a golf ball over the Open Cut, which is a mile wide, a mile long and 1,250 feet deep, so it's a can't-miss hole in one.

Mountain bike rentals are also available at the Sanford Lab Homestake Visitor Center. Several trailheads are just minutes away from the facility.

NEAT TO KNOW: THE STORY OF BLACK HILLS GOLD

Legend has it that the inspiration for the Black Hills gold design dates back to 1876 when a French goldsmith named Henri LeBeau came to the Black Hills to seek his fortune in gold. Unfamiliar with the region, LeBeau became lost, but to avoid starvation, he found wild grapes to eat. After being rescued, LeBeau realized that this experience was a sign and decided to make his fortune by recreating the grape and leaf clusters through jewelry designs, which he sold to other miners and prospectors. Today, Black Hills gold jewelry, with the distinctive tricolor grape cluster and leaf design in pink, green and yellow, can only be manufactured in the Black Hills of South Dakota. It is South Dakota's official state jewelry and sold throughout the world. Many stores throughout the Black Hills offer extensive collections of Black Hills gold.

For a special tour that shows how the region's famous Black Hills gold jewelry is made, visit **Mt. Rushmore Black Hills Gold Outlet Store & Factory Tours** at 2707 Mount Rushmore Road (US Hwy. 16) in Rapid City. It's open year-round, but call (605) 343-7099 in advance for tour times. Admission is free. For more details, visit www.blackhillsgold.com.

More Tours That Teach

25 SIOUX POTTERY

Take a self-guided tour and watch local artisans design and paint clay pottery. An adjacent gift shop offers an extensive collection of artists' handcrafted work for sale, including dreamcatchers and other specialty items with beadwork and quillwork.

> Open year-round; Free admission; 1441 E St. Joseph St., Rapid City, SD 57701; (800) 657-4366; www.siouxpottery.com

26 BLACK HILLS GLASS BLOWERS

Using heat and glass, these artisans create colorful handblown works of art, including vases, bowls, animals, ornaments and goblets. The showroom, which is located one mile west of the lone traffic light in Keystone, is open daily during the summer, but there aren't always glass-blowing demonstrations going on. Call ahead to confirm dates of blowing demonstrations.

> Open mid-May through mid-September; Free admission; 909 Old Hill City Rd. (1 mile west of Keystone), Keystone, SD 57751; (605) 666-4542; www.blackhillsglassblowers.com

NEAT TO KNOW

In Deadwood, **Mind Blown Studio** is located in a retro Texaco Station one block off Main Street. Spectators can watch molten glass transformed into glass sculptures. Classes are also offered. Glassware is available for sale, and the studio shares its space with a coffee bar and a deli. Call (605) 571-1071 or visit www.mindblowstudio.com.

27 PRAIRIE BERRY WINERY

This is a stop for the over-21 crowd. The family-owned winery includes a tasting room, gift shop and offers information about the wine-making process. They specialize in using local fruits, such as buffaloberry, chokecherry and rhubarb, for their award-winning wines that are released under the Prairie Berry label. Specialty jams, honey, coffee and other food items are also offered. Fresh sandwiches, pizza and other treats are available from the on-site deli, and an outdoor patio with a view of Black Elk Peak (formerly called Harney Peak) is the perfect place to sit and enjoy lunch. Next door, **Miner Brewing Company** is operated by the same entrepreneurial family and offers a variety of craft beers.

> Open year-round; Free admission; 23837 US Hwy. 385, Hill City, SD 57745; (877) 226-9453; www.prairieberry.com

CHAPTER 5

Meaningful Museums

Want to know about the Gold Rush Days in the Black Hills? Or learn more about the man who carved Mount Rushmore? Museums throughout the Black Hills tell these and other stories through an array of exhibits and collections. There's something to interest everyone, with museums dedicated to geology, American Indian culture, the Wild West, gold rush history, homesteading, motorcycles and military airplanes, just to name a few. These tributes to history give meaning to the region's past and present.

Old West Heritage

The history of mining, logging, ranching, education and pioneer life has been preserved in the turn-of-the-century artifacts on display at these museums.

28 THE JOURNEY MUSEUM & LEARNING CENTER

This comprehensive museum makes a great starting point for a trek back in time to learn about the geology of the Black Hills region. It covers a huge range of time—from the age of the dinosaurs all the way up to the geology and archaeology of the Great Plains, when pioneers and American Indians peopled the land. Museum exhibits include interactive rock and fossil displays, an archaeology timeline, a special fossil dig box for kids, and many pioneer and American Indian artifacts. Short films about the geology and cultures of the region are presented at regular intervals in the theater. The gift shop features an extensive collection of regional books and American Indian art. Throughout the year, special events—from concerts and speakers to kids' classes—are also offered at the museum.

Open year-round; Admission charged; 222 New York St., Rapid City, SD 57701; (605) 394-6923; www.journeymuseum.org

29 ADAMS MUSEUM

Artifacts tied to Deadwood and the Black Hills' pioneer past are on display in this three-level historical museum. The museum was founded in 1930 by local businessman W. E. Adams for the purpose of preserving the history of the Black Hills. You'll see a one-of-a-kind plesiosaur fossil, the original Thoen Stone (see Chapter 8, page 110), one of the largest gold nuggets found in the area, and learn about the colorful characters who called Deadwood home. Writers for the HBO series *Deadwood* used the museum's extensive collection of photographs and archival records to lend authenticity to the award-wining drama. A Western history bookstore on the main level provides many titles that share in-depth stories of Deadwood's past.

Open year-round; Admission by donation; 54 Sherman St., Deadwood, SD 57732; (605) 578-1714; www.deadwoodhistory.com

NEAT TO KNOW

The Homestake Adams Research and Cultural Center (HARCC) at 150 Sherman Street, Deadwood, preserves and provides public access to one of the nation's largest collections of Black Hills archival materials. Its collection includes photographs, maps, diaries and journals, as well as gold exploration and production reports, and more. Throughout the year, HARCC also hosts events, including reenactments, films, lectures and other activities. Learn more at www.deadwoodhistory.com or call (605) 722-4800.

Throughout Deadwood, Wild Bill Hickok is immortalized in bronze

30 HISTORIC ADAMS HOUSE

The Historic Adams House is an elegant, 1892 Queen Anne-style home with many of its original furnishings intact. Guided tours detail the history of two of Deadwood's founding families. Harris and Anna Franklin built the home, which was then purchased by W. E. Adams, founder of the Adams Museum in 1920. It was one of the first homes in the area to have modern conveniences such as plumbing, electricity and telephone service. In 1934, after Adams' death, his second wife, Mary, locked up the house and it sat vacant for almost 60 years. The home was purchased by the Deadwood Historic Preservation Commission in 1992—with many original items found just as they had been left. Today, visitors can step back in time and marvel at the oak interiors, hand-painted canvas wall coverings, stained glass windows and stories of the home's former occupants.

Open year-round; Admission charged; 22 Van Buren St., Deadwood, SD 57732; (605) 578-3724; www.deadwoodhistory.com

31 DAYS OF '76 MUSEUM

Over 60 authentic horse-drawn carriages, covered wagons and stagecoaches, including the original Deadwood Stagecoach, are on display, along with clothing and other memorabilia from the Days of '76 celebration, which has been held annually since 1924. It is located adjacent to the Days of '76 Rodeo Grounds, where the annual rodeo is held during the third weekend in July.

Open year-round; Admission charged; 18 Seventy Six Dr., Deadwood, SD 57732; (605) 578-1657; www.deadwoodhistory.com

32 BORGLUM HISTORICAL CENTER

This museum collection is dedicated to Gutzon Borglum, the artist who sculpted Mount Rushmore. Carvings and paintings that he created during his lifetime are on display, including a replica of Lincoln's gigantic eye on the mountain. Outside the museum is a duplicate of Borglum's "Seated Lincoln" bronze statue. The original was commissioned in 1910 and sits in front of the Essex County Courthouse in Newark. Children are sure to enjoy climbing on Lincoln's lap for a photo.

Open May through October; Admission charged; 342 Winter St., Keystone, SD 57751; (605) 666-4448; www.visitrapidcity.com/things-to-do/attractions/borglum-historical-center

NEAT TO KNOW

Gutzon Borglum also designed the torch on the Statue of Liberty in New York City.

33 KEYSTONE HISTORICAL MUSEUM

Housed in the old Keystone school, which was built in 1900 and used until 1988, this museum collection includes a variety of antique furniture and details the gold mining and Mount Rushmore carving history of the area. Memorabilia from Carrie Ingalls (sister of author Laura Ingalls Wilder) is also on display. Carrie lived in Keystone and operated a newspaper in the early 1900s. The museum even touts a bathtub used by President William Howard Taft.

Open July through mid-September; Admission by donation; 410 3rd St., Keystone, SD 57751; (605) 666-4494; http://keystonehistory.com

NEAT TO KNOW

The **"Old Town" Keystone Walking Tour** features 19 historical points from Keystone's early years. Sights include a log schoolhouse, an icehouse and a mercantile store. Printed brochures with information about each point are available at the **Keystone Museum**, and information panels are on display at each of the sites.

34 HIGH PLAINS WESTERN HERITAGE CENTER

Ranch and rodeo memorabilia on display here honor cowboys, pioneers and American Indians from the region. Also on display are authentic mining and blacksmith artifacts as well as a Deadwood-Spearfish stagecoach, chuckwagon, buggies and sleighs. A Pioneer Room depicts scenes from a completely furnished log cabin and schoolhouse as they would have looked a century ago. Outside is a display of antique farm and ranch equipment. From its balcony, the museum offers panoramic views of three states: South Dakota, Wyoming and Montana.

Open year-round; Admission charged; 825 Heritage Dr. (I-90 Exit 14), Spearfish, SD 57783; (605) 642-9378; www.westernheritagecenter.com

NEAT TO KNOW

The glass atrium of the High Plains Heritage Center building is designed to be similar to that of the National Cowboy and Western Heritage Museum in Oklahoma City.

35 OLD FORT MEADE MUSEUM

Established in 1878, this frontier post in the Black Hills was home to Lieutenant Colonel George Armstrong Custer's ill-fated 7th Cavalry Regiment. The museum shows a brief film, providing an overview of fort life and the history of Custer's 1874 Black Hills Expedition. It was here that the Star-Spangled Banner became the official music for military retreat, long before it became our National Anthem. The only survivor of Custer's "Last Stand" at the Little Bighorn was the horse Comanche; the animal was retired with military honors at Fort Meade and lived there for 10 years. Be sure to stroll the well-kept military grounds—now home to a veteran's hospital—where some of the fort's original buildings remain intact. Old Post Cemetery is the only original Cavalry Post Cemetery in the country that has not been moved to a new location. Adjacent to Fort Meade is a Bureau of Land Management recreational area, great for hiking or horseback riding.

Open May through October; Admission by donation; 55 Sherman St., Sturgis, SD 57785; (605) 347-9822; www.facebook.com/fortmeade/

NEAT TO KNOW

Black Hills National Cemetery, two miles east of Sturgis (I-90 Exit 34), is often called "The Arlington of the West." Dedicated in 1948, simple white headstones mark the final resting place for more than 20,000 veterans and their descendants who are buried here. The grounds are open daily from sunrise to sunset. For more details, call (605) 347-3830 or visit www.cem.va.gov/cems/nchp/blackhills.asp.

36 TRI-STATE MUSEUM

Exhibits include more than 5,000 artifacts from early pioneer settlers in the tri-state area of South Dakota, Montana and Wyoming, as well as rodeo history from the region's well-known cowboys. Belle Fourche annually hosts the Black Hills Roundup Rodeo over the Fourth of July. The museum is located adjacent to the Geographic Center of the Nation Monument (see Chapter 8, page 110).

Open year-round; Admission by donation; 415 5th Ave., Belle Fourche, SD 57717; (605) 723-1200; www.thetristatemuseum.com

37 FALL RIVER PIONEER MUSEUM

Displays showcase pioneer life and include everything from an early post office and a country store to a schoolhouse and a dentist office. Located in a nineteenth-century sandstone schoolhouse.

Open May through September; Admission charged; 300 N Chicago St., Hot Springs, SD 57747; (605) 745-5147; www.pioneer-museum.com

38 1881 CUSTER COUNTY COURTHOUSE MUSEUM

This original courthouse and jail features photos from Lieutenant Colonel George Custer's 1874 Black Hills Expedition, along with historical mining and Indian and schoolhouse artifacts. Three outbuildings include a carriage house, an outhouse and a hand-hewn log cabin.

Open May through September; Admission charged; 411 W Mount Rushmore Rd., Custer, SD 57730;(605) 673-2443; www.1881courthousemuseum.com

NEAT TO KNOW : HOW ABOUT AN OLD-TIME PHOTO?

If your museum trek has made you wild about life in the West a hundred years ago, try capturing the moment by posing for an old-time photo. Several small studios throughout the Black Hills specialize in recreating the Wild West in vintage portraits with you as the star. Costumes range from hardy pioneers to dance hall girls to law-abiding sheriffs to blushing brides. Youngsters look quite cute sitting in a washtub.

Woody's Wild West Old Time Photo

Open year-round; 641 Main St., Deadwood, SD 57732; (605) 578-3807; www.woodyswildwest.com

Sturgis Photo & Gifts

Open year-round; 1081 Main St., Sturgis, SD 57785; (605) 347-6570; sturgisphoto.net

Buffalo Old Time Photo Co.

Open May through October; 309 Main St, Hill City, SD 57745; (605) 574-3314; www.buffalophoto.net

Professor Samuel's Portrait Emporium

Open mid-April through September; 118 Winter St. (on Main Street), Keystone, SD 57751; (605)343-4267; www.profsamuels.com

GoodTyme Photo

Open mid-April to mid-September; 804 US Hwy. 16A, Keystone, SD 57751; (605) 666-4619; www.facebook.com/GoodtymePhoto/

American Indian Culture

39 TATANKA: STORY OF THE BISON

A picturesque mountain surrounded by the Black Hills is the perfect outdoor setting for this larger-than-life bronze statue, which depicts 14 bison being pursued over a cliff by three American Indian horseback riders. Sculpted by South Dakota artist Peggy Detmers, Tatanka is one of the largest bronze sculptures in the world. The work was commissioned by actor Kevin Costner, who filmed his award-winning movie *Dances With Wolves* in South Dakota.

Bronze buffalo amidst Native American horseback riders are breathtaking atop this Black Hills mountain near Deadwood

Visitors can enjoy the outdoor views and natural surroundings here. Displays in the visitor center tell the story of the bison on the Northern Plains through photographs and artifacts and underscore the importance of the bison to the American Indians' way of life. A snack bar and an American Indian gift shop are also on site.

Open mid-May through September; Admission charged; 100 Tatanka Dr. (1 mile north of Deadwood), Deadwood, SD 57732; (605) 584-5678; http://storyofthebison.com

40 VORE BUFFALO JUMP

This archaeological site is a natural sinkhole used by Plains Indians from the 1500s to the 1800s as a big game kill site. The Plains Indians led stampeding herds over the cliff, making the meat and furs easy to collect at the base of the cliff. Archaeologists say the remains of 20,000 bison are likely to be excavated at the Vore Jump. Presently, the site is open to the public during summer months.

An exhibit building is being developed at the site to aid research, education and cultural activities.

Open June through Labor Day; Admission charged; From I-90 take Exit 205 (eastbound) or Exit 199 (westbound), then take the access road north of I-90; PO Box 369, Sundance, WY 82729; (307) 266-9530; www.vorebuffalojump.org

IMPORTANT TO KNOW

Eighty miles south of Wall, South Dakota, on the Pine Ridge Indian Reservation, the tragic **Wounded Knee Massacre** occurred in 1890. Relations between the U.S. government and the American Indian people had been gravely strained over the years as settlers and gold miners moved into the Black Hills and the government seized lands inhabited by the native people. The confrontation that ensued on December 29, 1890, left a reported 150 Lakota men, women and children dead—some historical accounts put the number as high as 300. Today, a somber monument and signage at the Wounded Knee Cemetery pay tribute to those who lost their lives. Note that the monument is located on the Pine Ridge Indian Reservation in a remote area. While it is accessible year-round, consideration should be given to weather conditions before making the journey. Additionally, there is no direct driving route to Wounded Knee and some roads are gravel. A suggested route is to travel south of Wall to Scenic, within Badlands National Park, and then follow BIA Road 27. A Wounded Knee Museum is being planned in Wall, South Dakota.

Modern-Day Memorabilia

41 SOUTH DAKOTA AIR AND SPACE MUSEUM

Over 30 vintage military aircraft are on display here—from historic World War II bombers to the modern-day B-1. Exhibits are housed indoors and outside and also include General Eisenhower's personal B-25 transport from World War II, a H-13 helicopter and a Minuteman II Missile Launch Control Center. Free tours of the museum are available. Bus tours of Ellsworth Air Force Base and a Minuteman missile silo are also offered and depart from the museum daily from mid-May to mid-September. Aviation items are available for sale in the gift shop.

Open year-round; Free admission; 2890 Rushmore Dr. (I-90 Exit 67B if eastbound and Exit 67 if westbound; 7 miles east of Rapid City), Ellsworth AFB, SD 57706; (605) 385-5189; www.sdairandspacemuseum.com

42 SOUTH DAKOTA STATE RAILROAD MUSEUM

If you like trains, head here. This museum relates how railroads influenced South Dakota and America. Model trains, interactive displays and a 75-foot TimeRail mural are among the highlights.

Open mid-May through mid-October; Admission charged; PO Box 1070 (next to the 1880 Train depot), Hill City, SD 57745; (605) 574-9000; www.sdsrm.org

43 STURGIS MOTORCYCLE MUSEUM AND HALL OF FAME

As host to the Sturgis Motorcycle Rally and Races held early each August, it is fitting that Sturgis is also home to a museum dedicated to motorcycles. On display you'll see rare and extraordinary motorcycles and scooters from the early 1900s through modern day. With over 100 motorcycles in its collection, displays are rotated regularly, offering repeat visitors something new each time they stop in.

Open year-round; Admission charged; 999 Main St., Sturgis, SD 57785; (605) 347-2001; www.sturgismuseum.com

NEAT TO KNOW

In 1938, Sturgis hosted its first dirt-track motorcycle race; it has now evolved into the annual motorcycle rally, one of the largest in the world.

On your way to or from the Black Hills from the east, consider a stop at the **Pioneer Auto Show** along I-90 at Murdo, South Dakota. Over 250 collectible cars, motorcycles and antique tractors are on display, including the General Lee from *The Dukes of Hazzard*. Open year-round; admission charged. For more information visit www.pioneerautoshow.com or call (605) 669-2691.

NEAT TO KNOW: MOVIE MEMENTOS

In Deadwood's **Celebrity Hotel** at 629 Main Street, authentic movie props, costumes and vehicles are on display throughout the main floor, adding to the celebrity ambiance. Popular items include the Volkswagen "Herbie" from *The Love Bug*, Evil Knievel's jump bike, Jethro's outfit from *The Beverly Hillbillies* and Tom Hanks' high school yearbook, as well as items once worn by John Wayne, Elvis, Merle Haggard and Dolly Parton. A dozen guitars signed by their former famous owners are on display in the Guitar Bar. Call (605) 578-1909 or visit www.celebritycasinos.com.

Additional movie memorabilia can be found across the street at **The Mint Casino**. Here, John Wayne's pickup and prop guns used in classic Western movies are displayed. Visit 638 Main Street or call (605) 578-1201.

Also on Main Street is the **Midnight Star**. Owned by actor Kevin Costner, this establishment showcases collectibles from his career. The second level of the building operates as Diamond Lil's Sports Bar and Grill, and its walls are filled with displays of photos, costumes, props and movie posters from Costner's roles in *The Bodyguard, Bull Durham, Field of Dreams, Open Range* and much more. Call (605) 578-1555 or visit www.themidnightstar.com.

44 DAHL ARTS CENTER

History surrounds visitors as they view the Dahl's unique 180-foot oil-on-canvas panorama, which spans 200 years of U.S. economic history. The cyclorama mural was painted by Bernard Thomas, and special lighting and narration on site relate much of the nation's history—from the time of the first settlers on the East Coast to modern times. Additional exhibits and galleries in the Dahl focus on contemporary art. Special art and educational classes and concert events are offered throughout the year.

Open year-round; Admission by donation; 713 7th St., Rapid City, SD 57701; (605) 394-4101; www.thedahl.org

Cyclorama is a 180-foot panorama depicting 200 years of U.S. economic history

45 NATIONAL GRASSLANDS VISITOR CENTER

Here, you'll learn about the prairie plants, animals and natural resources that surround the Badlands area and make up the Buffalo Gap National Grasslands. The site also discusses Great Plains history, management and recreational activities on the National Grasslands, and there are interpretive displays and videos about the region.

Open year-round; Free admission; 708 Main St., Wall, SD 57790; (605) 279-2125; www.fs.usda.gov/detail/nebraska/specialplaces/?cid=stelprdb5228870

NEAT TO KNOW

At 531 Main Street in Wall, the **Wildlife Museum and Gift Shop** showcases a diverse collection of taxidermied animals from around the region and the world. Open mid-May through October. Call (605) 279-2418 for more information.

FOR MORE MUSEUM COLLECTIONS, SEE ALSO:

Chapter 1: National Presidential Wax Museum, Keystone, page 14; Indian Museum of North America, Crazy Horse Memorial (near Custer), page 18; Saloon No. 10, Deadwood, page 21

Chapter 3: Black Hills Institute of Geological Research Museum & Everything Prehistoric Gift Shop, Hill City, page 38; Museum of Geology, Rapid City, page 38

Chapter 4: Black Hills Mining Museum, Lead, page 45

CHAPTER 6

Outdoors to Explore

If you like to hike, bike, horseback ride, fish, camp—or simply relax—the Black Hills are a perfect destination. The beauty of the Black Hills National Forest is the backdrop for peaceful settings like the Mickelson Trail, Custer State Park, Bear Butte, Devils Tower and Spearfish Canyon. There are also several unique caves to explore. A listing of available boat, bicycle, horse, ATV, and even motorcycle rentals are listed in this chapter, along with information for winter sports, including skiing, snowboarding and snowmobiling. No matter the season, the Black Hills offer an endless variety of scenery and activities.

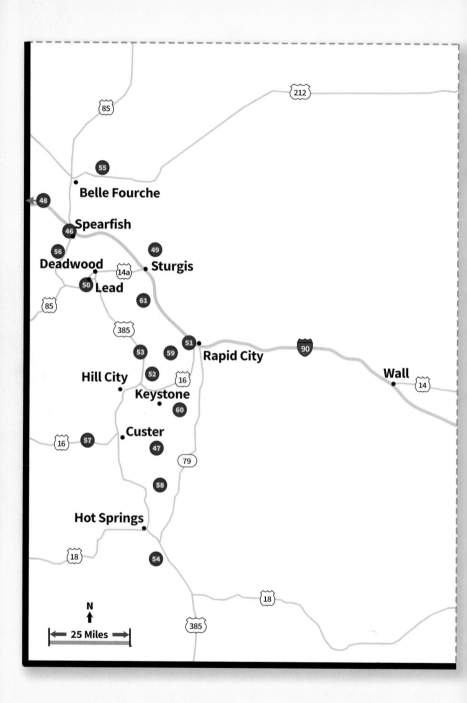

85

212

55

Belle Fourche

48

46 Spearfish

56

49

Deadwood

14a

Sturgis

50 Lead

61

85

385

53

59

51

90

Rapid City

Wall

52

14

Hill City

16

Keystone

60

16

57

Custer

47

79

58

Hot Springs

18

54

N

18

25 Miles

385

Scenic Settings

Lakes You'll Love

Cavernous Curiosities

By Bike, Horse or ATV

Scenic Settings

46 SPEARFISH CANYON

This picturesque canyon stretches for 20 miles along Spearfish Creek and is framed by towering canyon walls of limestone. With each changing season, the canyon presents a new perspective. Frank Lloyd Wright visited in 1933 and said, "Had Spearfish Canyon been on the 'throughway' to westward migration, the canyon would be as significant in public appreciation as the Grand Canyon is today."

Several waterfalls throughout Spearfish Canyon make it a picture perfect setting

The Canyon's Highway—US Hwy. 14A—is a National Scenic Byway that winds between Spearfish Canyon Golf Course and historic Deadwood. There are many turnouts for taking photos along the way, and sightseers are joined by fishermen, picnickers, bicyclers, joggers and hikers. Making your way along the highway, **Bridal Veil Falls** will catch your eye with its cascading water over the face of a 40-foot-high cliff.

At **Savoy**, Latchstring Village includes a restaurant and the stately **Spearfish Canyon Lodge**. Depending on the season, bicycles, snowshoes or snowmobiles can be rented at the resort's sport center. Creeks within the canyon offer year-round fishing; fly-fishing information is available through the lodge. Call (605) 584-3435 or (877) 975-6343, or visit http://spfcanyon.com.

A marked hiking trail that begins behind the Latchstring Inn descends down toward the creek and reveals breathtaking views of **Spearfish Falls**. Along the trail, signs identify local flora and provide a brief history of the Burlington Northern Railroad line that once ran directly over the top of the falls. West of Savoy and up Little Spearfish Canyon, **Roughlock Falls** is a popular picnicking and hiking spot with a trail that winds along Spearfish Creek and offers picturesque views of the waterfalls. About a mile beyond Roughlock Falls is the site where several scenes for the movie *Dances With Wolves* were filmed.

Accessible year-round; US Hwy. 14A, Spearfish, SD 57783; www.blackhillsbadlands.com/drives/spearfish-canyon-scenic-byway

NEAT TO KNOW

Along Spearfish Canyon at the intersection of US Hwy. 85 and US Hwy. 14A is **Cheyenne Crossing**, so named because it is the point where the old Cheyenne Trail crossed Spearfish Creek. This is a popular stop thanks to its gift shop and a restaurant that serves up homemade pancakes, Indian tacos and burgers perfect for those with big appetites. Open daily May through October, and weekends November through April. Call (605) 584-3510 or visit www.cheyennecrossing.org. Next door, **Wickiup Cabins** offers log cabins for rent year-round. Call (605) 584-3382 or (800) 505-8268, or visit www.spearfishcreekcabins.com.

47 CUSTER STATE PARK

Hiking, mountain biking, rock climbing, swimming, canoeing, paddleboating and trail rides are just a few of the many reasons visitors call Custer State Park a favorite. The park's herd of 1,300 bison roams freely throughout the park, along with a variety of other wildlife that includes everything from pronghorn antelope, elk and wild turkeys to mountain goats and bighorn sheep.

Initially established as a game reserve in 1913, the area was dedicated as Custer State Park in 1919 by former South Dakota Governor Peter Norbeck. Today, it is home to an education center and the 70-mile **Peter Norbeck Scenic Byway**, which encircles the park and showcases much of its natural beauty. The Peter Norbeck Outdoor Education Center hosts a variety of educational programs for all ages throughout the summer. View details at https://gfp.sd.gov/state-parks/directory/custer/activities/educational.aspx.

To get to know the park, stop at one of the park's three visitor centers where you can pick up maps and learn about the many trails, nature areas, lakes and educational programs. For overnight stays, there are nine campsites and five resorts within Custer State Park—some even offer cabins year-round—but reservations are necessary. Call (800) 710-2267 for camping and (888) 875-0001 for the resorts.

Open year-round; Admission charged; 13329 US Hwy. 16A, Custer, SD 57730; (605) 255-4515; www.custerstatepark.info

FAVORITE HIKING TRAILS WITHIN CUSTER STATE PARK

If hiking is your fancy, many trails within Custer State Park offer panoramic views. In addition, mountain biking and horseback riding are allowed in most areas of Custer State Park unless otherwise posted. For detailed trail information visit https://gfp.sd.gov/state-parks/directory/custer/trails/hiking-biking.aspx.

The summit of Black Elk Peak is capped with stone steps and an observation tower

The most popular hike is the trek to the top of **Black Elk Peak**. Formerly called Harney Peak, this is the state's highest point, topping out at 7,242 feet. The tallest mountain between the Rockies and the Swiss Alps, the summit affords a panoramic view of four states. Trail 9 and Trail 4 at **Sylvan Lake** both lead to Black Elk Peak. Trail 9 is 3 miles one way, and it's the easiest and most-traveled route. Trail 4 is 3.25 miles one way and goes from Sylvan Lake to the **Little Devil's Tower** trailhead and then on toward the peak. A round-trip journey on either of these trails takes about 4 hours and is moderately strenuous.

OTHER TRAILS INCLUDE:

Easy: These trails mainly follow level ground.

Sylvan Lake Shore Trail is a 1-mile loop that encircles Sylvan Lake. Most of the trail is flat, but a portion crosses rocky areas.

Creekside Trail is a 2-mile, paved, handicapped-accessible trail that follows Grace Coolidge Creek between the State Game Lodge and Coolidge General Store.

Moderate: Parts of these trails follow steep slopes and rocky areas.

Badger Clark Historic Trail is located behind the historic Badger Hole, the home of the late Charles Badger Clark, South Dakota's first poet laureate. This trail makes a 1-mile loop through the forest and rocky hillside.

Prairie Trail makes a 3-mile loop off the Wildlife Loop Road. This trail features prairie grasslands and wildflowers.

Stockade Lake Trail begins on the southeast side of Stockade Lake and ascends to a ridgeline where excellent views of the area can be seen. The trail makes a 1.5-mile loop.

Little Devil's Tower Trail begins 1 mile east of Sylvan Lake on Needles Highway. The 3-mile, one-way trail leads to the unique rock formation known as Little Devil's Tower. The summit also provides beautiful views of the Cathedral Spires and Black Elk Peak.

Strenuous: Much of these trails follow steep slopes and rocky areas.

Sunday Gulch Trail begins behind the dam at Sylvan Lake and follows a 2.8-mile loop into the forest. The trail offers spectacular scenery of granite walls and wild streams.

Lovers Leap Trail is a popular trail that begins behind the schoolhouse across from the Peter Norbeck Visitor Center. The trail makes a 3-mile loop and follows the top of a ridgeline, with a rocky outcrop at the highest point called Lovers Leap. Mount Coolidge, Black Elk Peak and the Cathedral Spires can be viewed from this high point. The trail does include some creek crossings, which can be challenging.

Cathedral Spires Trail is a one-way, 1.5-mile trail to the rugged granite spires. The trailhead begins 2.5 miles east of Sylvan Lake on Needles Highway.

NEAT TO KNOW: ON THE ROCKS

The Black Hills region is quickly becoming recognized for the outstanding rock climbing that its granite spires offer. Favorite formations for climbers to conquer include the Devils Tower National Monument near Hulett, Wyoming, the Needles Eye in Custer State Park, the granite peaks near Mount Rushmore and the limestone cliffs in Spearfish Canyon. A long-time guide service in the region is **Sylvan Rocks**. Call (605) 484-7585 or learn more at www.sylvanrocks.com.

CULTURE TO EXPLORE

Cultural activities within Custer State Park include the **Badger Hole**, the historic log cabin home of Charles Badger Clark (1883–1957), South Dakota's first poet laureate. After a cabin tour, hike the Badger Clark Historic Trail and reflect at quiet stops among the pines. Open Memorial Day through Labor Day.

At the **Gordon Stockade**, near Stockade Lake, you can see a replica of the log fort built by the Gordon party who came to this area in search of gold in 1874. A reminder of the early Gold Rush days, interpretive signs explain the story of the Gordon party. Accessible year-round. Stockade Lake offers camping, boating and fishing.

Also during the summer, the **Black Hills Playhouse** offers live theater productions in the park. Nightly performances begin at 7:30 p.m.; Wednesday and Sunday matinees are at 2 p.m. Call (605) 255-4141 or visit www.blackhillsplayhouse.com for information and tickets.

RESORTS & RECREATION

The park's five resorts are hubs of activity and feature everything from swimming and boating opportunities to Buffalo Jeep Rides and chuckwagon cookouts. The resorts in Custer State Park also offer their own unique restaurants with offerings ranging from casual burgers to more upscale items such as trout, pheasant and bison. For details about each lodge, visit www.custerresorts.com or call (888) 875-0001.

Sylvan Lake Resort is a popular attraction because of the soothing lake of the same name nearby. Here, visitors can picnic, swim, fish, go boating, climb among the granite rocks, meander along the trail that encircles Sylvan Lake or hike one of the many trailheads that begin here. The lodge's stately design was influenced by Frank Lloyd Wright. Because of its scenic setting, this is a popular spot for weddings. In addition to the restaurant and lodge rooms, amenities include cabins for rent, banquet facilities, a campground, convenience store and boat rentals. Call (605) 574-2561.

Legion Lake Resort is located on the water's edge and offers fishing, canoe, kayak and stand-up paddleboard rentals, plus a sandy beach for lounging. You can rent cabins here, or just take a hike around the lake or on the nearby Centennial Trail. You can even pick up a fishing license and supplies at the Legion Lake General Store. The Legion Lake Restaurant offers breakfast and casual food items such as burgers, pizza, sandwiches and salads. Call (605) 255-4521.

Blue Bell Lodge and Resort is known for its western flair, including guided trail rides, hayrides and chuckwagon cookouts where guests even get a cowboy hat and a bandanna as souvenirs. Some cabins are available here year-round. The

Blue Bell Lodge Dining Room features Western classics such as bison, steak, fish, and even rattlesnake sausage.

The historic **State Game Lodge and Resort** was nicknamed the "Summer White House" after hosting Presidents Coolidge and Eisenhower. The historic presidential rooms are open for viewing at set hours; they can also be reserved for overnight stays. Buffalo Safari Jeep Rides leave from the State Game Lodge and allow visitors to get into the backcountry of the park. Nearby, several specialty cabins are available for rent year-round.

Built in 2008, **Creekside Lodge** is the newest lodging addition to Custer State Park and offers modern, oversized lodge rooms. It does not have its own restaurant, but is located near the historic State Game Lodge for access to its full-service restaurant. Open year-round.

Buffalo Roundup at Custer State Park

FOR MORE ABOUT THE WILDLIFE WITHIN CUSTER STATE PARK, SEE ALSO:

Chapter 2: Custer State Park, page 27

NEAT TO KNOW: MORE MUST-SEE ATTRACTIONS IN CUSTER STATE PARK

US Hwy. 16A, also known as the **Iron Mountain Road**, provides spectacular views of Mount Rushmore and the Black Hills. The winding mountain road features three tunnels that were constructed specifically to frame views of Mount Rushmore, and three famous corkscrew bridges, which are also called pigtail bridges.

Two geological features in Custer State Park include the famous Needles Eye and the Cathedral Spires, both of which can be viewed along **Needles Highway**. These outcroppings are made of granite. From the right viewpoint, Needles Eye appears to be a gigantic sewing needle. The Cathedral Spires resemble a massive set of organ pipes set into the mountain scenery.

The **Mount Coolidge Lookout and Fire Tower** was built in 1940 by the Civilian Conservation Corps atop a 6,023-foot peak. It is used both for communications and spotting fires. Visitors can hike or drive to the top of Mount Coolidge, and then climb the lookout tower to see views of Mount Rushmore, Crazy Horse Memorial, Black Elk Peak, the Needles formations, and on a clear day, the Badlands, which are over 60 miles away. The turnoff to the tower is located on SD Hwy. 8, where a 1.7-mile gravel road winds up the mountain. The road is not well suited for large vehicles or motor homes.

The **French Creek Natural Area** and **Grace Coolidge Walk-In Fishing Area** have been designated as natural areas and will be left untouched by human development. Between them, they offer great fishing and wildlife viewing.

Custer State Park's **Coolidge General Store** was built in 1927 to accommodate the entourage of staff, reporters and curious tourists who followed President Coolidge to the park's State Game Lodge, where he stayed that summer. The structure was built by shipbuilders from Minnesota. Once you're inside the store, be sure to look up; the builders used their ingenuity to craft a ceiling that resembles the hull of a ship turned upside down.

48 DEVILS TOWER NATIONAL MONUMENT

In 1906, President Teddy Roosevelt designated the 1,267-foot tall Devils Tower as the nation's first national monument; in the original proclamation, the apostrophe in "Devil's" was left out, and the name stuck. The unique structure is actually a core of lava that hardened near sedimentary rock; over millions of years the soft rock weathered away, exposing the Devils Tower. A 1.3-mile paved walking path encircles the base of the tower. The area also offers marked hiking trails, rock climbing (by permit), summer cultural programs and camping. For more information, check out the visitor center. Night sky viewing is popular at the monument and ranger-led astronomy programs are held at the amphitheater every Sunday night throughout the summer.

Monument open year-round; Admission charged; PO Box 10 (9 miles west of Hulett, WY), Devils Tower, WY 82714; (307) 467-5283; www.nps.gov/deto

NEAT TO KNOW: THE LEGEND OF DEVILS TOWER

According to one telling from American Indian lore, the mountain was created when seven small girls chased by a bear jumped on a rock and prayed to the rock to save them. The rock heard their pleas and began to elongate itself upward, pushing them higher, out of the bear's reach. The bear clawed and jumped at the sides of the mountain, but broke its claws and fell to the ground. The little girls were pushed up into the sky, where they are to this day in a group of seven little stars, the Pleiades. The marks of the bear's claws are seen as the vertical ridges on Devils Tower.

49 BEAR BUTTE STATE PARK

Considered sacred ground by American Indians, Bear Butte stands alone on the plains east of Sturgis. *Mato Paha*, or bear mountain, is the Lakota name given to the unique formation. It is not a flat-topped butte, as its name implies, but a single mountain rising up from the prairie.

Wildlife abounds in these wild places

Bear Butte served as a landmark that helped guide settlers and gold prospectors into the region after Lieutenant Colonel George Custer camped near the mountain and verified rumors of gold in the Black Hills. Today, Bear Butte State Park has been designated as a National Natural Landmark and a National Recreation Trail. The popular hiking trail winds nearly two miles up to the summit of Bear Butte, where you'll discover a breathtaking view of four states. During your hike, you may also get glimpses of native wildlife and the small herd of buffalo that roams at the base of the mountain.

The Bear Butte Education Center, located near the park entrance, offers interpretive displays about the geological story of the site, its significance as a pioneer landmark and its continuing role as a holy mountain for several Indian tribes. The center is open May through September.

Bear Butte Lake, across the highway from Bear Butte, offers a pretty setting for a picnic. A 2.5-mile trail encircles the lake. Campsites, a boat ramp and a handicap-accessible fishing dock are also available.

Open year-round; Admission charged; 20250 SD Hwy. 79, PO Box 688, Sturgis, SD 57785; (605) 347-5240; https://gfp.sd.gov/state-parks/directory/bear-butte/

NEAT TO KNOW: SACRED GROUND

Among American Indians, the Black Hills are considered a sacred, holy place where the great spirits live. *Paha Sapa* is the native people's name for the area; very loosely translated, it means "black hills," a name that stems from how black the pine-covered slopes look from a distance. Notable Lakota leaders, including Red Cloud, Crazy Horse and Sitting Bull, all visited Bear Butte, and many American Indians still hold religious ceremonies on the mountain. During your visit, you may see colorful prayer cloths and tobacco ties hanging from the trees; these represent the prayers offered by individuals during their worship.

Bear Butte State Park is linked to Custer State Park and Wind Cave National Park by the 111-mile **Centennial Trail** that winds through the Black Hills. It is open to hikers, mountain bikers, horseback riders and cross-country skiers. See https://gfp.sd.gov/state-parks/directory/custer/docs/centennial-trail-brochure.pdf for more details.

50 GEORGE S. MICKELSON TRAIL

Named for the late South Dakota governor who supported it, the 109-mile Mickelson Trail winds through the heart of the Black Hills and follows the historic Burlington Northern Railroad line from Deadwood to Edgemont. Passing pine trees, granite outcroppings, stands of aspen and spruce, quiet meadows and gurgling streams, the trail is popular with hikers, cyclists and horseback riders, and it's also a favorite for cross-country skiing or snowshoeing in winter.

The trail has 15 trailheads in all, and it features everything from gentle slopes to extreme treks, not to mention tunnels, bridges and more amid the beautiful backcountry. The trail winds through several towns—and ghost towns—with 30 interpretive signs along the way to explain special features. For bicycle rentals, see page 79.

Accessible year-round; A user fee is charged; 11361 Nevada Gulch Rd., Lead, SD 57754; (605) 584-3896; http://gfp.sd.gov/state-parks/directory/mickelson-trail/

NEAT TO KNOW: FIND NEMO

The scenery surrounding the tiny town of Nemo is breathtaking. Situated in a peaceful valley in the heart of the Black Hills National Forest, Nemo was the site of William Randolph Hearst's first logging operation in 1876, which supplied lumber to the Homestake Mine in Lead. The **Nemo Guest Ranch** offers cabins, RV hook-ups and campsites. Located on Nemo Road off US Hwy. 385 south of Deadwood. Call (605) 578-2708 or visit www.nemoguestranch.com.

51 OUTDOOR CAMPUS—WEST

An oasis within Rapid City, this facility includes an educational learning center, surrounded by a natural area offering 1.5 miles of trails to explore. A small lake allows opportunities for fishing and canoeing. Educational programs are offered for all ages throughout the year.

Accessible year-round; Free admission; 4130 Adventure Tr., Rapid City, SD 57702; (605) 394-2310; https://gfp.sd.gov/outdoor-learning/outdoor-campus/west/default.aspx

FOR MORE AREAS TO HIKE AND EXPLORE, SEE ALSO:

Chapter 3: Badlands National Park, page 36

Lakes You'll Love

Many picturesque lakes are found throughout the Black Hills, offering family fun for fishing, swimming and boating. A number of lakes are mentioned in this chapter, and other popular spots include:

52 SHERIDAN LAKE

Located north of Hill City, beside US Hwy. 385, Sheridan Lake is the second-largest lake in the Black Hills National Forest. It has a sandy, westward-facing beach that many consider the sunniest in the Black Hills. The area offers two campgrounds, three picnic areas, hiking trails (including the Flume Trail and the Centennial Trail) and ample fishing. Sheridan Lake Marina operates from mid-May through mid-October. Pontoon boats, canoes, paddleboats and kayak rentals are all available. Wave runners are also allowed on the lake. Some ice fishing is done in January and February. A vacation rental home is available year-round. Call the marina at (605) 574-2169 or visit http://sheridanlakemarina.com.

53 PACTOLA LAKE

At 860 acres, the Pactola Reservoir is the largest lake in the Black Hills National Forest and up to 158 feet deep. The man-made lake is backed up behind Pactola Dam and used for flood control on Rapid Creek, which flows through Rapid City. The Pactola Visitor Center (open Memorial Day through Labor Day), just south of the dam on US Hwy. 385, provides a scenic overlook of the lake and information about the Black Hills National Forest.

The lake has marinas on both its north and south sides, and it also features boat ramps and rents pontoon and fishing boats, as well as canoes, kayaks and paddleboards. Water skiing, cliff diving, and even scuba diving are popular activities nearby. Three picnic grounds and two campgrounds are also located on the lake. Pactola Pines Marina is open from April 15 through October 15, with limited hours before Memorial Day and after Labor Day. Call the marina at (605) 343-4283 or visit www.pactolalake.com and www.pactolapines.com.

54 ANGOSTURA RESERVOIR RECREATION AREA

This man-made lake is a haven for those who yearn to be on the water, and it has ample room for boating, fishing and swimming, as well as 36 miles of shoreline with some of the finest sand beaches in South Dakota. Fishermen will enjoy catching walleye, smallmouth bass, crappie, and on occasion, northern pike, largemouth bass, perch and bluegill. The recreation area is a great spot for picnics and includes playgrounds, hiking and biking trails and four campgrounds. Paddleboard and cabin rentals are also available on site. Located 10 miles southeast of Hot Springs on US Hwy. 385/18.

Open year-round; Admission charged; 13157 N Angostura Rd., Hot Springs, SD 57747; (605) 745-6996; https://gfp.sd.gov/state-parks/directory/angostura/

55 ORMAN DAM AND ROCKY POINT RECREATION AREA

Located eight miles east of Belle Fourche on US Hwy. 212, this 8,000-acre reservoir was created in 1911 when Orman Dam was constructed to store water for agricultural use. When it was completed, it was the largest earthen dam in the world, and in 1989 was designated a National Historic Civil Engineering Landmark. Today, it is a popular camping, boating and fishing destination. Amenities also include a swimming beach, playground, camping cabins and picnic shelters.

Open year-round; Admission charged; 18513 Fishermans Rd., Belle Fourche, SD 57717; (605) 641-0023; http://gfp.sd.gov/state-parks/directory/rocky-point

56 IRON CREEK LAKE

Located 20 miles south of Spearfish via a gravel road, this quiet lake in the northern Black Hills offers a sandy beach, swimming, fishing, and paddleboat rentals. Hiking, biking and volleyball are popular, as are the lake's rustic cabins and a primitive campground for RVs and tents. A general store operates Memorial Day through Labor Day and offers snacks and other necessities on site.

20912 Iron Creek Lake Rd., Spearfish, SD 57783; (605) 642-5851; www.ironcreeklake.com

OTHER LAKES AND STREAMS

Smaller lakes with campgrounds include **Roubaix Lake**, which also has a nice sandy beach (south of Deadwood off US Hwy. 385), and **Horsethief Lake** (along SD Hwy. 244 near Mount Rushmore). **Center Lake** and **Bismarck Lake** in Custer State Park are also popular fishing spots.

Within Rapid City, **Canyon Lake** is popular. See page 94 for more information.

Keyhole State Park, southwest of Devils Tower in Wyoming and accessible from I-90, offers a large reservoir for fishing, boating and water sports and has several campgrounds. Visit http://wyoparks.state.wy.us/Site/SiteInfo.aspx?siteID=10.

Rainbow trout are the most abundant trout species found in Black Hills lakes, while brown and brook trout are mostly found in streams. **Deerfield Lake** is 15 miles northwest of Hill City and boasts some of the best trout fishing in the region. Visit www.fs.usda.gov/recarea/blackhills/recreation/recarea/?recid=26203&actid=29.

If it's trout streams you're after, check out **Rapid Creek, French Creek** and the spring-fed **Spearfish Creek**. Rapid Creek originates west of Rapid City and continues east, eventually flowing through the city. Spearfish Creek in Spearfish Canyon is one of the most scenic fishing areas in the Black Hills and offers a good supply of rainbow trout. French Creek flows through Custer State Park in the Southern Black Hills.

Note: *Fishing licenses are required in South Dakota. Visit http://gfp.sd.gov/fishing-boating/fish-licenses.aspx for details.*

NEAT TO KNOW: CATCH OF THE DAY

For guaranteed fishing success, cast your line at **Trout Haven**, located 20 miles south of Deadwood and 19 miles west of Rapid City on US Hwy. 385. No license is needed, and Trout Haven furnishes the fishing rod and bait. The experience is fun for all ages, and the on-site Pier Café will fry your catch immediately or pack your trout on ice to go. The café serves breakfast, lunch and dinner. Cabins and RV spots are also for rent. Open Memorial Day through early October. Call (605) 341-4440 or visit https://www.facebook.com/trouthavenresortsd.

Cavernous Curiosities

Want to know what the Black Hills are really made of? Get an in-depth geology lesson with an underground tour of one of the region's unique caves. A ring of limestone encircles the land beneath the Black Hills, and the region is home to a number of impressive caves. All of the caves offer guided, public tours showcasing rare underground crystal formations such as stalactites, stalagmites, boxwork and cave popcorn. These caverns make an especially good place to visit on bad-weather days or during heat waves because most stay a constant temperature of about 50° F.

57 JEWEL CAVE NATIONAL MONUMENT

With over 180 miles of mapped passageways, Jewel Cave is the third-longest cave in the world. Overseen by the National Park Service, the cave gets its name from the jewel-like crystals that line its walls; visitors can get an up-close look at these features on the scenic cave tours, which are given several times daily. Special "wild caving" tours are offered but require a reservation and strenuous activity. Hiking is also offered on three surface trails that surround the national monument.

Open year-round; Admission charged; 11149 US Hwy. 16 (12 miles west of Custer on US Hwy. 16), Custer, SD 57730; (605) 673-8300; www.nps.gov/jeca

58 WIND CAVE NATIONAL PARK

Named for the strong wind currents found within it, Wind Cave offers five different tours of its extensive passageways. The less strenuous tours are a half-mile long, while longer tours last from two to four hours and include as many as 450 stairs. Reservations are available for some of the tours, as well as for large groups.

Get underground by taking a caving tour

Above ground, Wind Cave is surrounded by more than 28,000 acres of native grasslands and Ponderosa pine forests that offer 30 miles of hiking trails, as well as camping and picnic areas. Horseback riding is also permitted. The fire lookout tower at the summit of the **Rankin Ridge Trail** (1.25 miles long) offers a panoramic view of the Black Hills. The park can be accessed from US Hwy. 385 (10 miles north of Hot Springs) or on SD Hwy. 87 from Custer State Park.

Open year-round; Admission charged; 26611 US Hwy. 385, Hot Springs, SD 57747; (605) 745-4600; www.nps.gov/wica

59 BLACK HILLS CAVERNS

Black Hills Caverns feature over a dozen different types of crystal formations—from nailhead spar crystals to soda straw stalactites. Two guided tours are offered on site, and the gift shop has rare rocks, crystals and other collectibles.

Open mid-May through September; Admission charged; 2600 Cavern Rd. (4 miles west of Rapid City on SD Hwy. 44), Rapid City, SD 57702; (605) 343-0542 or (800) 837-9358; http://blackhillscaverns.com

West of Black Hills Caverns on SD Hwy. 44 (10 miles west of Rapid City) is another underground marvel—a subterranean waterfall. Located 600 feet inside of what once was a Black Hills gold mine, **Thunderhead Underground Falls** is sure to take your breath away. The hike to see the waterfall is easily accessible. Open May 1 through September; admission charged. For information, contact (605) 343-0081.

60 RUSHMORE CAVE

The closest cave to Mount Rushmore and easily accessible, Rushmore Cave offers beautiful views of nature's underground creations. Highlights include the floral room where stalactites seem to create budding leaves and floral designs, and the big room, where you'll see cave bacon and more stalactites than in any other place in the Black Hills. Reservations for special Xpedition Adventure tours—which require some belly crawling through tight spaces—are available from June through mid-August. The Rush Mountain Adventure Park is operated in conjunction with the cave and features several "thrill rides" on site. For more information about that attraction, see page 92.

Open year-round; Admission charged; 13622 SD Hwy. 40 (6 miles east of Keystone), Keystone, SD 57751; (605) 255-4384; www.rushmorecave.com

61 WONDERLAND CAVE

Located in the heart of the Black Hills National Forest, it's a scenic drive to reach this historic cave, which has been open to the public since 1929. To get there, take I-90 Exit 32 at Sturgis and follow the signs along Vanocker Canyon Road.

Open May through October; Admission charged; Nemo, SD 57759; (605) 578-1728; www.southdakotacaves.com

By Bike, Horse or ATV

BICYCLE RENTALS

For a bicycle tour of the Hills, bring your own bike or rent one at any of the several rental locations available along the 109-mile Mickelson Trail (see page 74). Many offer tour packages and shuttle services with drop-off and pick-up points.

Mickelson Trail Adventures
Rentals and shuttle services available April to October; 24024 S US Hwy. 16/385, Hill City, SD 57745; (605) 574-4094; www.mickelsontrailadventures.com

Rabbit Bicycle
Rentals April to October; Shuttle services and overnight lodging packages available; 175 Walnut Ave., Hill City, SD 57745; (605) 574-4302; www.rabbitbike.com

DeadWheels

Rentals May through September; Shuttle services and variety of bikes available; 32 Charles St., Deadwood, SD 57732; (402) 689-2682, www.deadwheelsbikerentals.com/

Spearfish Canyon Lodge

Rentals May through September; The Little Spearfish Trail and Rimrock Trail are also popular destinations; 10691 Roughlock Falls Rd., Lead, SD 57754; (605) 584-3435 or 877-975-6343; http://spfcanyon.com/experience/mountain-biking

---

NEAT TO KNOW: MOTORCYCLE RENTALS

If you prefer a motorcycle to a bicycle, you can rent one—provided that you have a motorcycle license and proof of insurance. Rentals are available through **Black Hills Harley Davidson** in Rapid City. Call (800) 727-2482 or visit www.blackhillshd.com for more details. In Sturgis, contact **EagleRider** at (605) 206-7832 or visit www.eaglerider.com/sturgis.

Exploring the Black Hills on horseback only makes sense

TRAIL RIDES

Saddle up at one of these trail ride locations and explore the Black Hills the traditional way—on horseback. Tour packages range from just one hour to day-long rides.

The Stables at Palmer Gulch

One- to two-hour trail rides are offered and there are three trails to choose from. Evening rides to and from a chuckwagon dinner are also available.

Available Memorial Day through Labor Day; Between Keystone and Hill City on SD Hwy. 244, (605) 574-3412; http://ridesouthdakota.com/rushmore-horseback-riding/

Blue Bell Lodge Stables

Located within Custer State Park, excursions of one to two hours are offered. Half-day and full-day rides are also available, and they include lunch.

Available Memorial Day to mid-September; (605) 255-4700; http://custerresorts.com/activities/activities-in-the-park/guided-trail-rides

High Country Guest Ranch

Rides are offered several times throughout the day and feature scenic views of the Black Hills National Forest.

Available Memorial Day to mid-September; 12138 Ray Smith Dr., Hill City, SD 57745; (605) 574-9003; http://highcountryranch.com

Rockin' R Trail Rides

Hourly and half-day rides are available and provide a unique view of the Crazy Horse Memorial.

Available Memorial Day weekend through September; Heritage Village, 24853 Village Ave., Custer, SD 57730; (605) 673-2999; www.rockingrtrailrides.com

ATV RENTALS

All-terrain vehicle (ATV) riders will find 650 miles of designated roads and trails to explore in the Black Hills National Forest. A few areas are off-limits, and these include Spearfish Canyon, Black Elk Wilderness, and the Mickelson Trail. The USDA Forest Service offers complimentary maps showing where Off-Highway Vehicle (OHV) travel is permitted. Learn more at www.fs.usda.gov/activity/blackhills/recreation/ohv or from local rental places, including the following:

Black Hills Off-Road Rentals

21399 US Hwy. 385 (located near Steel Wheel Campground), Deadwood, SD 57732; (605) 584-4777; www.blackhillsoffroadrentals.com

High Country Guest Ranch

12138 Ray Smith Dr., Hill City, SD 57745; (605) 574-9003; http://highcountryranch.com

Recreational Springs Resort

11201 US Hwy. 14A, Lead, SD 57754; (605) 584-1228; http://recreationalspringsresort.com

Mt. Meadow Campground and Resort

11321 Gillette Prairie Rd., Hill City, SD 57745; (605) 574-2636; www.mtmeadow.com

Mad Mountain Adventures

21433 US Hwy. 385, Deadwood, SD 57732; (605) 578-1878; www.madmountainadventures.net

Mystic Hills Hideaway

21766 Custer Peak Rd., Deadwood, SD 57732; (605) 584-4794; www.mystichillshideaway.com

Trailshead Lodge

22075 US Hwy. 85, Lead, SD 57754; (605) 584-3464; www.trailsheadlodge.com

Black Hills Outdoor Fun

Available May through September; Only guided tours are offered; 12780 Black Forest Rd., Rapid City, SD 57702; (605) 574-2430; www.blackhillsoutdoorfun.com

WINTER DELIGHTS

With its annual abundant snowfall, the Black Hills are transformed into an ideal winter getaway. The area offers two ski resorts, 350 miles of groomed snowmobile trails, cross-country skiing, and even ice fishing.

Downhill Skiing

Deer Mountain Ski Resort

With over 50 mountain trails, Deer Mountain is the perfect place for downhill skiing and snowboarding. Triple and double chairlifts provide access to the 6,850-foot summit. The **Zero Gravity Tube Park** is fun for all ages as you speed down the snow-covered hill on an inner tube. A convenient towrope will pull you to the top of the hill for your next ride. The on-site lodge offers a café and pub, as well as a fireplace and TV. Equipment rental and ski lessons are also available.

11187 Deer Mountain Rd., Lead, SD 57754; (605) 580-1169; www.deermtnsd.com

Terry Peak Ski Area

With the summit of Terry Peak standing at 7,100 feet tall, it has the distinction of being the highest lift service between the Rockies and the Swiss Alps. With four high-speed chairlifts, over 20 miles of groomed trails, and a terrain park with a half-pipe and a variety of jumps and rail features, it has more than enough to keep skiing and snowboarding enthusiasts entertained. The "snow carpet," a moving sidewalk installed at the base of the bunny hill, provides a great way to get up the hill for young and beginning skiers before they tackle the chairlift. **Stewart Lodge** offers equipment rentals, a cafeteria and lounge, a retail store, and a ski school where lessons are offered for all ages. The smaller **Nevada Gulch Lodge** offers food and beverages. Lift tickets can be purchased at both lodges.

21120 Stewart Slope Rd., Lead, SD 57754; (800) 456-0524 or (605) 584-2165; www.terrypeak.com

Snowmobiling

Find trails and conditions at http://gfp.sd.gov/to-do/snowmobile/.

Black Hills Off-Road Rentals

21399 US Hwy. 385 (near Steel Wheel Campground, Deadwood, SD 57732; (605) 584-4777; www.blackhillsoffroadrentals.com

Recreational Springs Resort

11201 US Hwy. 14A, Lead, SD 57754; (605) 584-1228;
http://recreationalspringsresort.com

Spearfish Canyon Lodge

10691 Roughlock Falls Rd., Lead, SD 57754; (605) 584-3435 or (877) 975-6343;
http://spfcanyon.com/experience/snowmobiling-in-spearfish-canyon

Mt. Meadow Campground and Resort

11321 Gillette Prairie Rd., Hill City, SD 57745; (605) 574-2636; www.mtmeadow.com

Mad Mountain Adventures

21433 US Hwy. 385, Deadwood, SD 57732; (605) 578-1878;
www.madmountainadventures.net

Mystic Hills Hideaway

21766 Custer Peak Rd., Deadwood, SD 57732; (605) 584-4794;
www.mystichillshideaway.com

Trailshead Lodge

22075 US Hwy. 85, Lead, SD 57754; (605) 584-3464; www.trailsheadlodge.com

Ice Skating

Roosevelt Park Ice Arena (indoor)

Offered September through May; Skate rental on site; 235 Waterloo St., Rapid City,
SD 57701; (605) 394-6161; www.rcgov.org/departments/parks-recreation/
ice-arena.html

Main Street Square (outdoor)

Offered mid-November through February; Skate rental on site; 512 Main St.,
Rapid City, SD 57701; (605) 716-7979; http://mainstreetsquarerc.com

CHAPTER 7

Water Parks, Go-Carts and Other Good Times

Create fun family memories at modern-day adventure parks that feature everything from water parks and mini-golf to go-carts, old-time steam engines, ziplines, and even hot air balloons. Or, spend a leisurely afternoon at Storybook Island, one of the Black Hills' premier parks.

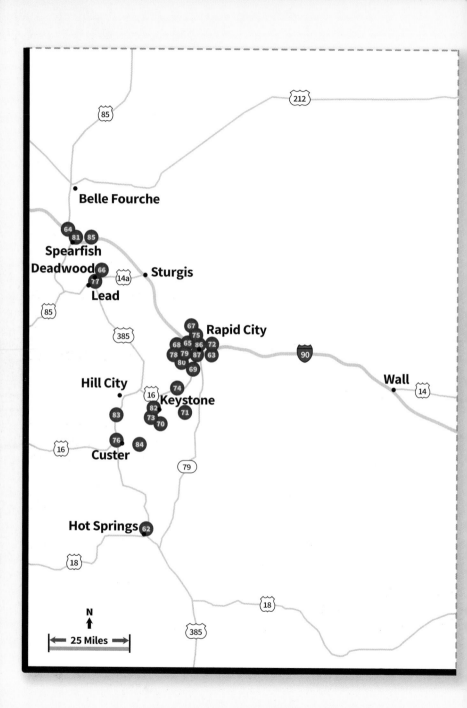

Wonderful Water Parks

Great Go-Carts & Amusement Parks

Magnificent Mini-Golf

Perfect Parks

Thrill Rides

Wonderful Water Parks

62 EVANS PLUNGE MINERAL SPRINGS

Established in 1890, Evans Plunge is the oldest tourist attraction in the Black Hills, and one of the largest natural warm water indoor swimming pools in the world. The natural spring-fed waters maintain an average pool temperature of 87° F. The venue entertains all ages with its waterslides, tubes, Tarzan rings, and two kiddie pools, each with their own frog-themed slide.

At Hot Springs, take the plunge in thermal mineral water that's 87°

The facility stands where it was originally founded in 1890. Built over a group of small springs and one giant thermal spout of warm mineral water, water flows up through the pebble bottom of the pool at a rate of 5,000 gallons per minute, ensuring fresh, clean water at all times; the water is not treated with chlorine. The facility includes two hot tubs heated to 104° F, and an outdoor pool open during the summer months.

Open year-round; admission charged; 1145 North River St. (on the north side of Hot Springs off US Hwy. 385), Hot Springs, SD 57747; (605)745-5165; www.evansplunge.com

NEAT TO KNOW: HOT SPRINGS HISTORY

Originally called Minnekahta, or *wiwila kata* by the Lakota, meaning "warm waters," the town's name was changed to Hot Springs in 1886. The large, rose-colored sandstone buildings that still line Hot Springs' charming streets were built in the late nineteenth century as elaborate hotels to pamper the throngs of people who came to play and be healed by the therapeutic, warm spring waters of the town. The mineral water contains calcium, potassium, lithium, magnesium, manganese and naturally occurring hydrogen peroxide, which pioneers believed to be useful in the treatment of chronic diseases and in relieving arthritis. Today, the sandstone structures, built from the rock of the surrounding ridges, have been renovated to include antique shops, restaurants, hotels, museums, and—true to the town's history—bathhouses and spa services.

The **Red Rock River Resort Hotel & Spa** occupies one of the grand sandstone buildings designed over a century ago. Today, the modernized resort offers a relaxing retreat with its hotel rooms and on-site spa services. Open year-round. Call (605) 745-4400 or visit www.redrockriverresort.com.

63 WATIKI INDOOR WATERPARK RESORT

With over 30,000 square feet of pool space, this facility delivers summer fun all year long. The facility includes several waterslides, a lazy float river, a hot tub and an arcade. Adding to the fun, the adjacent Sliders Bar and Grill restaurant features a see-through waterslide right in the center of the dining area. For guests wanting to stay on site, there are three adjacent hotels: La Quinta Inns & Suites, Fairfield Inn & Suites and Residence Inn by Marriott.

Open year-round; Admission charged; 1416 N Elk Vale Rd. (I-90 Exit 61), Rapid City, SD 57703; (877) 545-2897; www.watikiwaterpark.com

64 SPEARFISH REC & AQUATIC CENTER

What once was a Walmart is now a popular recreation center, with the 2-acre outdoor water park as the pièce de résistance. It features three huge waterslides, a pool-side climbing wall, a lazy river, a 400-gallon dump bucket and a kiddy pool. Indoors, the 71,000-square-foot facility, which was modified in 2008, offers a double gymnasium and a variety of workout rooms. A food and beverage concession operates on-site.

Pool open June through Labor Day; Recreation facility open year-round; Admission charged; 122 Recreation Dr., Spearfish, SD 57783; (605) 722-1430; http://spearfishreccenter.com

Cool off on Spearfish Aquatic Center's three huge waterslides

65 FOUNTAINS AT MAIN STREET SQUARE

The interactive fountains at Rapid City's Main Street Square are a big attraction, and they delight all ages during the summer months. The water dances and plays to a set routine as squealing children, and a few daring adults, weave in and out of the surprising spouts. Be sure to bring a towel, because if you stroll through the fountains, you will get wet! If you decide to spend the day at the Main Street Square, the surrounding shops provide a variety of fun shopping and eating options as well. And in the evening, lights illuminate the fountain sprays, making it a unique show worth seeing.

Open mid-May through mid-October; No admission fee; 526 Main St., Rapid City, SD 57701, (605) 716-7979; http://mainstreetsquarerc.com/fountains.html

NEAT TO KNOW:

Main Street Square in downtown Rapid City is a destination all its own. Throughout the year, a variety of events are hosted, from concerts and festivals to holiday-themed events such as the spring Eggstravaganza, Halloween's Scare in the Square, and the Holiday Celebration and Winter Market. Winter activities also include converting a portion of the square into public ice skating. No matter the time of year, the Main Street Square brings people of all ages together. Call (605) 716-7979 or visit http://mainstreetsquarerc.com.

66 INDOOR WATER PLAYLAND AT THE LODGE AT DEADWOOD

A killer whale slide, a giant waterfall mushroom, a lily pad water walk, a pirate ship and poolside water squirt guns help keep families entertained at this hotel's indoor pool. The lodge is connected to a large casino and convention area and offers two restaurants on the premises: **Oggie's Sports Bar** and the upscale **Deadwood Grille**.

Open year-round; Free for registered hotel guests; 100 Pine Crest Ln., Deadwood, SD 57732; (877) 393-5634; www.deadwoodlodge.com

67 INDOOR WATERPARK AT BEST WESTERN RAMKOTA HOTEL

This indoor pool is themed and surrounded by palm trees, a pirate ship, several kid-friendly slides, water cannons, and not one, but two, 165-foot flume waterslides. The Ramkota is also home to **Minerva's**, one of the area's best restaurants, and is conveniently located next to the **Rushmore Mall**, making this a great getaway destination anytime of year.

Open year-round; Free for registered hotel guests; 2111 N LaCrosse St. (I-90 Exit 59), Rapid City, SD 57701; (605) 343-8550; rapidcity.bwramkota.com

NEAT TO KNOW:

Located at 940 Sheridan Lake Road in Rapid City, the **Jimmy Hilton Municipal Pool** is no ordinary pool. It includes a family leisure pool, waterslides, lily pads, and even a dinosaur slide. Open June to mid-August. Call (605) 394-1894.

Rapid City's **Roosevelt Swim Center** at 125 Waterloo Street offers indoor swimming year-round with slides, a diving board and lanes for laps. Call (605) 394-5223.

Great Go-Carts & Amusement Parks

68 FLAGS AND WHEELS INDOOR RACING

High-energy entertainment is the name of the game at this indoor adventure park. Activities include go-carts on a 27,000-square-foot track, paintball, laser tag, bumper cars, batting cages and an arcade. This is the only facility in the state that also offers Extreme Race Karts, which can reach speeds of 40 mph; drivers must be at least 16 years of age and have a valid driver's license.

Open daily; Admission charged; 405 12th St. (take Omaha Street to 12th Street), Rapid City, SD 57701; (605) 341-2186; www.flagsandwheels.com

69 BLACK HILLS MAZE FAMILY ADVENTURE PARK

The main attraction at this family-friendly park is a 1.2-mile labyrinth of walkways, bridges, stairs and towers to navigate through. Additional entertainment includes bankshot basketball, batting cages, water balloon wars, a 25-foot climbing wall, racing scooters and mini-golf.

Open Memorial Day to Labor Day; Weekends only in May and September; Admission charged; 6400 US Hwy. 16 (3 miles south of Rapid City), Rapid City, SD 57701; (605) 343-5439; www.blackhillsmaze.com

70 RUSHMORE TRAMWAY ADVENTURES

Adventure awaits at this multifaceted attraction, which features an alpine slide, ziplining, a scenic chairlift ride, a free-fall tower and an aerial adventure park. Your biggest challenge may be deciding which activities to do. The chairlift ride up the mountain gives scenic views of Mount Rushmore. At the summit, you can enjoy the view, and even grab lunch or a cold drink at the Mountain-Top Grille. Then, catch the easy chairlift ride back down, or hop on a bobsled and ride down the thrilling 2,000 feet of track filled with dips, twists and turns. For the faint of heart, riders do have brakes to control their own speed.

For even more adventure, the double zipline spans 800 feet across an expanse of the scenic pine trees. The free-fall tower is 60 feet tall and promises an adrenaline rush. And finally, the aerial adventure park is essentially an obstacle course suspended amid the trees. Eight different ropes courses are featured, and there are levels for everyone, from first-timers to experts. The courses feature 80 platforms and integrate ziplines, bridges, ladders, rings, nets and more. It's a climbing adventure you won't soon forget.

Open May through September; Admission charged; 203 Cemetery Rd., Keystone, SD 57751; (605) 593-4913; www.rushmoretramwayadventures.com

71 RUSH MOUNTAIN ADVENTURE PARK

Rushmore Cave is the centerpiece of this Adventure Park (learn more about the cave on page 79), but a variety of adventure-themed attractions have been added to make this a destination that families can enjoy for several hours to an entire day. The Rushmore Mountain Coaster is the Black Hills region's only coaster of its kind, featuring one- and two-person carts that follow the suspended rails up inclines, around pigtail curves and then rushing downhill. Each individual rider can control the speed of their cart; daredevils have the ability to reach speeds of 30 mph. On the Soaring Eagle Zipline, riders accelerate 630 feet down the mountainside on a suspended cable. This zipline appeals to riders of all ages because instead of a hanging harness, riders sit in a formed seat with a seatbelt. And, side-by-side seats allow the option to experience the thrill ride with a friend. As a bonus, once riders zip to the bottom of the hill, this unique ride then pulls them back up the hill to their starting location. Also entertaining, the Gunslinger 7-D Interactive Ride offers a multisensory experience. With laser guns, moving seats and other surprise effects, it's a fun game of shooting targets and competing for the highest score—and bragging rights. Gemstone Mining is another attraction here. Kids get hands-on experience in the sluice box, sifting for fossils, arrowheads and various gems.

Open year-round; Hours vary with season; Admission charged; 13622 SD Hwy. 40, Keystone, SD 57751; (605) 255-4384; www.rushmorecave.com/rush-mountain-adventure-park/

72 JUMP CRAZE TRAMPOLINE PARK

Kids jump up and down with excitement—literally—at this unique indoor facility, which features a variety of trampolines. A series of launch platforms and angled walls allow jumpers to bounce from one zone to the next. Also popular is bouncing from the trampoline into the foam pits or bouncing high to score in the dunk zone. A toddler zone for jumpers under 46 inches tall is also available. All participants must sign a waiver. Package pricing and a party room for special events are also available.

Open year-round; Admission charged; 449 Americas Way, Box Elder, SD 57701; (605) 791-1728; http://jumpcrazeusa.com

Magnificent Mini-Golf

73 HOLY TERROR MINI-GOLF

Designed with a gold mine theme, this 18-hole course is set against a steep mountain and includes putting around a waterwheel, a millpond and mining sluices. The course is fully lighted and open until 9 p.m. during peak summer season.

Open May 15 through October 31; Fee charged; 609 US Hwy. 16A (next to the National Presidential Wax Museum), Keystone, SD 57751; (605) 666-5170; www.holyterrorminigolf.com

74 PUTZ-N-GLO

This indoor mini-golf course has a rock 'n' roll theme that lights things up with a black light and puts a new spin on the game by playing rock tunes from past decades. A snack bar and video arcade are also on site. Gemstone panning and a miner's maze adventure are also offered outside during the summer season.

Open daily May through Labor Day; Limited hours October through April; Fee charged; 23694 Strato Rim Dr. (2 miles past Bear Country on US Hwy. 16), Rapid City, SD 57702; (605) 716-1230; www.putznglo.com

75 PIRATE'S COVE

Try a challenging round of mini-golf at this 18-hole course centered around a pirate theme; it's complete with caves, waterfalls and an abandoned ship.

Open May through mid-October; Fee charged; 1500 LaCrosse St., Rapid City, SD 57709; (605) 343-8540; www.piratescove.net

76 GRIZZLY GULCH ADVENTURE GOLF

This is a rustic-themed course with plenty of obstacles to putt through, over and around.

Open May through early September; 231 W Mount Rushmore Rd., Custer, SD 57730; (605) 673-1708; https://www.facebook.com/Grizzly-Gulch-Adventure-Golf-719365871423235/

77 DEADWOOD 18-HOLE MINI-GOLF

Kids and adults will enjoy this scenic course, which features gazebos and fountains and offers scenic views of the surrounding Black Hills.

Open Memorial Day through early November; Admission charged; 225 Cliff St. (at the Comfort Inn & Suites), S US Hwy. 85, Deadwood, SD 57732; (605) 578-7550 or (800) 961-3096; www.deadwoodcomfortinn.com/deadwood-mini-golf

Perfect Parks

78 STORYBOOK ISLAND

This popular outdoor park has castles, a pirate ship, and even nursery rhyme characters. Dr. Seuss, Winnie the Pooh, Cinderella and over 100 other fairy tale characters are on display amid shaded picnic areas and playground equipment. The pint-sized children's train is a favorite for all youngsters; the same goes for the carousel and the children's theater; it features a variety of performances several times daily throughout the summer.

Open Memorial Day through Labor Day; Free admission; Nominal charge for train, carousel, theater and holiday events; 1301 Sheridan Lake Rd., PO Box 9196, Rapid City, SD 57709; (605) 342-6357; www.storybookisland.org

Noah's Ark is just one of the adorable stories come to life at Rapid City's Storybook Island

NEAT TO KNOW:

In December, Storybook Island is bedecked in Christmas lights for a walk-through wonderland. Santa greets children of all ages in the gift shop.

79 LEGACY COMMONS PLAYGROUND AT MEMORIAL PARK

Kids can climb, twist and spin at this interactive modern-day playground. Separate play areas are designed for different age groups and feature sensory play, educational play and exercise play. Themes include rock- and rope-climbing obstacle courses, nature discovery panels and a popular sway glider that can hold multiple people. Several areas are accessible by children of all physical capabilities. The playground is set amid scenic natural landscaping and is next to Memorial Park.

Accessible year-round; 600-684 Omaha St., Rapid City, SD 57701; (605) 716-7979; www.downtownrapidcity.com/legacy-commons.html

80 CANYON LAKE PARK

Located on the west side of Rapid City, this family-friendly setting allows visitors to feed ducks and geese, rent a paddleboat, stroll over the bridge to the gazebo on the island, or try their luck fishing. Numerous picnic and playground areas surround the area.

Canyon Lake Resort, located at 4510 Shore Drive, offers paddleboat rentals, as well as lodging. Call (605) 343-0234 or visit www.canyonlakeresortsd.com. Nearby at 2850 Chapel Lane, **Lake Park Campground** rents furnished cottages, as well as camping sites. Call (605) 341-5320 or visit www.lakeparkcampground.com.

Accessible year-round; 4181 Jackson Blvd., Rapid City, SD 57702; (605) 394-4175

81 SPEARFISH CITY PARK

Located along Spearfish Creek and adjacent to the D.C. Booth Historic Fish Hatchery (see page 30), this tree-filled park is a picturesque place to enjoy the outdoors. Feeding the fish at the hatchery is a favorite activity for young and older visitors alike. A paved path winds along the creek and meanders through the town, and it's perfect for walking or biking. A large, castle-like playground at the park will entertain kids for hours. On hot days, consider bringing your own inner tube to float along the shallow creek's cool waters. Fishing on the creek is also popular. **Spearfish City Campground** is within walking distance. Call (605) 642-1340. Bicycles can be rented at Rushmore Mountain Sports in Spearfish at 505 Main Street. Call (605) 642-2885 or visit www.rushmorebikes.com.

Accessible year-round; Canyon St., Spearfish, SD 57783; (605) 642-1333

FOR MORE PARKS, SEE ALSO:

Chapter 3: Dinosaur Park, Rapid City; page 38

Thrill Rides

For a one-of-a-kind way to view the beauty of the Black Hills, consider taking a train, a plane, a helicopter, or even a hot air balloon ride; unique jeep and trolley tours are also available. Whichever you choose, be prepared for the experience of a lifetime.

82 THE 1880 TRAIN AND BLACK HILLS CENTRAL RAILROAD

Hop aboard the 1880 Train at Hill City or Keystone to enjoy the scenery of the Black Hills from a vintage steam train, one of America's last steam trains still in service. The 20-mile, 2-hour round-trip follows the original route of the Chicago, Burlington & Quincy Railroad line, which was laid down in the late 1880s to service the mines and mills between Hill City and Keystone. En route you'll see vistas of the Black Hills National Forest and Black Elk Peak, South Dakota's tallest mountain. Reservations are required. Depots in both Hill City and Keystone feature gift shops with train memorabilia. Several special events—such as an Old West Shootout—are offered throughout the summer season, and ticket deals are available on holidays such as Mother's Day and Father's Day. In November and December, Holiday Express rides are offered. These are 1-hour round-trip rides from Hill City to the North Pole, and feature a special visit from Santa. Find details on the 1880 Train website under the Special Events tab.

May through early October; Admission charged; PO Box 1880, Hill City, SD 57745; (605) 574-2222; www.1880Train.com

---

NEAT TO KNOW:

While in Hill City to catch the 1880 Train, make a point to eat lunch or dinner at the well-known **Alpine Inn**. The restaurant is housed in the former Harney Peak Hotel building, which was built in 1886 and is a charming, historic landmark on Hill City's Main Street. The décor and lunch menu with a European flair were influenced by the German mother-daughter duo who opened the restaurant in 1984 and still operate it today. The popular dinner, served from 5 to 9 p.m., features two simple entrées: filet mignon, a lettuce wedge, baked potato and Texas toast or kaes-spaetzle primavera, a German-style pasta. And save room for dessert—over 30 delightful choices are offered. Open year-round; closed Sundays. Call (605) 574-2749 or visit www.alpineinnhillcity.com.

83 BLACK HILLS AERIAL ADVENTURES

A variety of helicopter tour packages are offered for high-altitude views of the Black Hills and Badlands; three heliport locations are operated: one near Badlands National Park, one near Keystone and one near Crazy Horse. View website for locations and directions.

Open mid-May through October; Fee charged; 24564 US Hwy. 16/385, Custer, SD 57730; (605) 673-2163; http://coptertours.com/

84 BLACK HILLS BALLOONS

Floating high above the earth in a hot air balloon, you'll see spectacular scenes of Custer State Park, scenic lakes and herds of wildlife. The balloon pilots are federally licensed, and flights take approximately an hour and are offered at sunrise. Advance reservations are required.

Offered May through October, Weather permitting; Fee charged; 25173 Lower French Creek Rd., Custer, SD 57730; (605) 673-2520; www.blackhillsballoons.com/

85 EAGLES' VIEW AIR TOURS

Enjoy the Black Hills scenery and monuments with a personal airplane tour. Package options include a 30-minute Deadwood and Spearfish Canyon tour, a 70-minute Devils Tower tour, an 80-minute Mount Rushmore tour, or a 2-hour "see it all" tour that includes Spearfish Canyon, Devils Tower, Mount Rushmore, Crazy Horse and Deadwood.

Tours offered year-round; Fee charged; 300 Aviation Pl, Spearfish, SD 57783; (605) 642-4112 or (800) 843-8010; www.eagleaviationinc.com

86 BLACK HILLS OPEN-TOP-TOURS

Touring the Black Hills is fun and full of fresh air in one of the many open-top vehicle options available through this touring company. There are about a dozen different styles of vehicles to choose from, including a convertible-top van, a 1953 Willys Wagon with a 6-foot removable roof, and a safari jeep with removable sides and top. The variety of private tour options throughout the Black Hills are as varied as the vehicles. Packages include visits to Mount Rushmore, Crazy Horse and Custer State Park. Fly fishing tours are also offered. During the winter months, SnoTrax 4x4 Utility Terrain Vehicles (UTVs) for 5 to 8 passengers are available for viewing wildlife in Black Hills scenery in the Northern Hills.

Available year-round; Fee charged; 302 Racine St., Rapid City, SD 57701; (605) 644-6736; http://blackhillsopentoptours.com

87 BLACK HILLS PARTY PEDALER

This is a group bicycle available for rent. With seats for up to 11 people (8 pedaling and 3 riding), there is also a staff "pilot" aboard who steers and operates the brakes to ensure safety. Rapid City tours begin and end at Hay Camp Brewing Company, 201 Main Street, Suite 109, and Spearfish tours begin and end at Crow Peak Brewing Company, 125 W US Hwy. 14. Riders can select a few stops along the 2-hour tour route they choose, and riders over age 21 can purchase alcohol at the starting points to bring on the ride. Riders may bring their own snacks and non-alcoholic beverages on the tour provided space is available. This party on wheels makes a memorable outing for birthday parties, youth groups, pub crawls, bachelor/bachelorette parties, and anyone wanting to have a fun time! In Rapid City, Pokemon Go Tours and Hope-a-Ride Tours are also offered at special times, which are announced via the website.

Available May through October; Fee charged; Rapid City, SD 57701; (605) 645-0435; www.bhpartypedaler.com

NEAT TO KNOW: TAKE A TROLLEY RIDE

In Deadwood, hop aboard one of the green trolleys that circle the town. They run at regular intervals between all the hotels and other popular locations in town, including the Adams Museum, Adams House, Days of '76 Museum and Rodeo Grounds, and Mount Moriah Cemetery. Cost is just $1 per ride, and trolleys operate 365 days a year. For more information, visit www.cityofdeadwood.com and select the Trolley tab.

In Rapid City, the **City View Trolley** offers a narrated tour of points of interest found throughout town. Trolley stops include The Journey Museum, Storybook Island, Dinosaur Park, and the Dahl Arts Center. The trolley operates June through August and the fare is $2 per adult and $1 for children. Riders may board at any of the trolley stop locations. Learn more at www.rapidride.org/city-view-trolley.

FOR OTHER FUN RIDES, SEE ALSO:

Chapter 1: Deadwood bus tours, page 20

Chapter 6: Hayrides and chuckwagon cookouts, Blue Bell Lodge, Custer State Park, page 67; Buffalo Safari Jeep Rides, State Game Lodge and Resort, Custer State Park, page 71; Trail rides, page 80; Bicycle rentals, page 79; ATV rentals, page 81; Snowmobile rentals, page 82

The Chuck Wagon Dinner Show

Hot air balloons are one unique way to enjoy the Black Hills

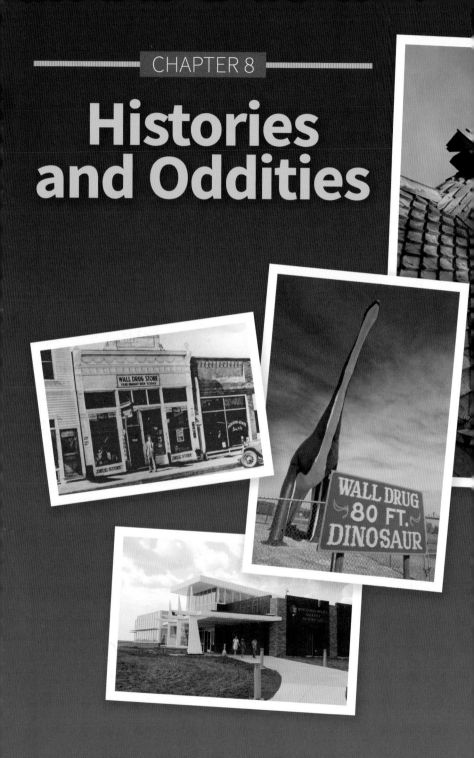

CHAPTER 8

Histories and Oddities

WALL DRUG
80 FT.
DINOSAUR

No vacation would be complete without unexpected detours and one-of-a-kind roadside attractions. And the Black Hills offer an array of unique destinations—from historical sites to bewildering wonders. Take time to visit some of these uncommon places and you may be surprised to find that they are among the highlights of your trip.

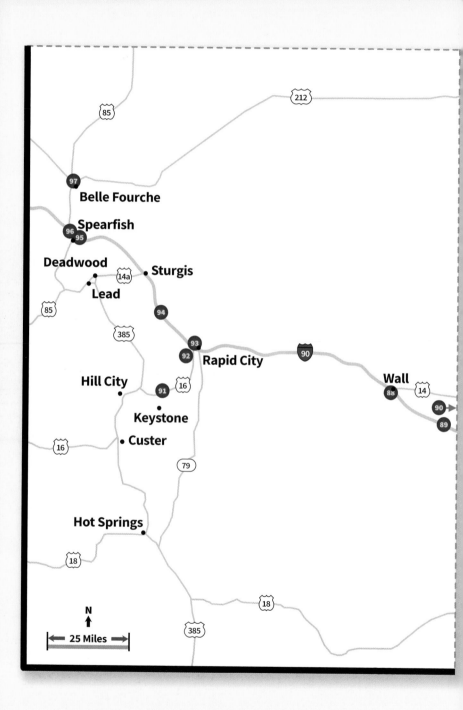

88 WALL DRUG

Once a simple small-town drugstore in the 1930s, Wall Drug has grown to become a shopping emporium complete with a Western art gallery and clothing store, a bookstore stocked with a varied selection by regional authors, a fudge shop, a rock shop, a jewelry store, and, of course, a myriad of kitschy items to fit every tourist's fancy, including a Jackalope, Turd Birds, T-shirts, and a popular selection of cowboy boots and hats.

Established in 1909, Wall Drug was just like any other pharmacy of its day, until it was purchased by Ted Hustead and his wife, Dorothy, in 1931. After five years of dismal business during the Great Depression, Dorothy had the idea to put up signs and billboards along the highway, offering free ice water at Wall Drug. The promotion soon attracted weary travelers en route to Mount Rushmore and other Western destinations, and shortly thereafter, Wall Drug was no longer just a pharmacy. The Western store, restaurant and souvenir merchandise were soon added to their offering.

Ted Hustead established Wall Drug in the 1930's; today it's a shopping emporium, consuming most if Wall's Main Street

In the decades since, the Wall Drug billboards can still be found around the globe—and many continue to promote free ice water. Today, the third generation of Husteads operates the gussied-up drugstore on Wall's Main Street. Open year-round, it still houses a pharmacy, but it mainly caters to tourists, with as many as 20,000 visitors a day stopping at Wall Drug during the peak summer season.

The restaurant still features five-cent coffee and homemade donuts; if you're there for dinner, try the buffalo burger and a slice of homemade pie. Also be sure to take a gander at the silver dollar collection in the restaurant's countertop, with dates ranging from 1878 to 1928.

Other don't-miss attractions include one of the best Western art galleries in the region, and several historical photographs, original paintings and sculptures on display throughout the complex—some by Mount Rushmore sculptor Gutzon Borglum and South Dakota native Harvey Dunn.

Amid the shopping you'll find memorabilia, wooden cowboy and Indian figures, and even a Travelers Chapel for a quiet moment of reflection. Wall Drug's Back Yard is geared toward children with its roaring *Tyrannosaurus rex*, a 6-foot rabbit, a buckin' horse to climb on, and, of course, the famous free ice water. Kids can also tour a replica of a gold mine and pan for their very own gems.

Open year-round; Free admission; 510 Main St., PO Box 401, Wall, SD 57790; (605) 279-2175; www.walldrug.com

89 MINUTEMAN MISSILE NATIONAL HISTORIC SITE

An eerie part of American—and world—history is preserved and open to the public at the Minuteman Missile National Historic Site. Operated by the National Park Service and located east of Wall on I-90, this was once a top-secret facility. From 1963 through the early 1990s, thousands of Air Force personnel were stationed in Minuteman Missile fields throughout the Great Plains. These sites kept nuclear weapons at the ready—24 hours a day, 365 days a year, for 30 years—in case any aggressor nation considered launching a nuclear attack against the United States or its allies. Intercontinental Ballistic Missiles (ICBMs), which were stored underground at the Minuteman sites, had ranges from 6,000 to 9,300 miles, making virtually any target in the world vulnerable.

South Dakota's Minuteman Missile National Historic Site allows visitors to see the actual facilities used for this mission and learn about the work done by the missile crews. The site is comprised of the Visitor Center, located immediately north of I-90 Exit 131, and two additional sites: the historic Launch Control Facility Delta-01 and the Launch Facility Delta-09, which are 4 miles and 15 miles, respectively, from the Visitor Center.

Ranger-led tours of the Delta-01 Launch Control Facility (located north of I-90 near Exit 127) are offered daily for a nominal fee. Advanced reservations are required and can be made online or by phone at (866) 601-5129. The 30-minute tours provide a walk-through of the grounds and the aboveground support building that was used by individuals stationed at the site. Then, tour participants descend 31 feet in the original elevator to enter the underground control center, where they can see the array of electronics that were used to monitor the deadly missiles. Tour participants must be physically capable of climbing two 15-foot ladders unassisted in the event of an elevator failure.

Minuteman Missile Silo Visitor Center

Self-guided tours of the Delta-09 facility (located south of I-90 near Exit 116) are offered via a cell phone audio recording, which can be accessed by calling (605) 301-3006. Delta-09 was a missile silo that contained a fully operational Minuteman Missile, bearing a 1.2-megaton nuclear warhead. The Delta-09 missile silo was one of 150 silos spread across western South Dakota. There are ten points along the audio tour that are marked by signs discussing the history of the site and the other Minuteman missile sites across the Great Plains region. Visitors can look down into the actual Delta-09 missile silo, which is protected by a glass viewing enclosure.

Within the Visitor Center, exhibits share stories of the technology that made nuclear weapons possible, the tales of the servicemen and women who manned these stations, and a good deal of information about this tumultuous time in history. In 1991, the Soviet Union collapsed, bringing the Cold War to an end, and Minuteman Missile sites were soon deactivated and decommissioned.

Open year-round; Tours offered for a nominal fee; Reservations required; 24545 Cottonwood Rd. (I-90 Exit 131), Philip, SD 57567; 605) 433-5552; www.nps.gov/mimi

90 1880 TOWN

Located 150 miles east of Rapid City on I-90 at Exit 170, the 1880 Town boasts an impressive collection of more than 30 original buildings built from the 1880s to the 1920s. A church, a town hall, a general store, a jail, a one-room schoolhouse, and a farmstead complete with barn and windmill are among the attractions. Each building is authentically furnished and includes displays of historical photos, effectively transporting visitors back in time. Additionally, the museum within the town showcases memorabilia that once belonged to world champion cowboy Casey Tibbs. *Dances with Wolves* movie props are on site and fun activities for kids, including mule-drawn wagon rides and costume rentals of Old West garb, are also available. A gift shop is featured in the 14-sided barn, and snacks and drinks are served in the saloon. Adjacent to the 1880 Town is a Conoco gas station and convenience store. The 1950s Train Diner operates in a real railroad car; it serves breakfast and lunch, and is well known for its homemade pies.

Open Memorial Day through Labor Day; Admission charged; PO Box 507; Murdo, SD 57559; (605) 344-2236; www.1880town.com

NEAT TO KNOW: TOWNS OF YESTERYEAR

Located four miles west of Custer along US Hwy. 16 (on the way to Jewel Cave), the aptly named **Four Mile Old West Town** offers visitors a firsthand look at the buildings, furnishings and artifacts of the past century. Audio recordings providing additional information about the buildings are available to enhance self-guided walking tours. Open Memorial Day through early October; admission charged. Call (605) 673-3905 or visit www.blackhillsbadlands.com/business/four-mile-old-west-town.

A classic general store from a century ago, the **Aladdin General Store** is complete with roll-top flour bins and the original counters. Now listed on the National Register of Historic Places, the store offers an assortment of T-shirts, caps and other clothing, as well as sweet treats for road-weary travelers. It's located west of Belle Fourche on SD Hwy. 34 on the way to Devils Tower, or 9 miles north of I-90 at Exit 199. Open year-round. Call (307) 896-2226 or visit www.facebook.com/pages/Aladdin-General-Store/197520763605727.

Rockerville was once a thriving community during the Gold Rush Days of the 1880s. Located 9 miles south of Rapid City on US Hwy. 16 and on the way to Mount Rushmore, its storefronts are all boarded up, creating something of a modern-day ghost town. Not everything is gone, however, as the bustling **Gaslight Restaurant and Saloon** is open in Rockerville and serves steaks, seafood, pasta and salads. Call (605) 343-9276 or visit www.thegaslightrestaurant.com/.

Rochford is another Black Hills town that was established in 1877 during the Gold Rush. It quickly grew to 200 houses and 500 people, but by 1900 it had only 48 residents. Today, visitors still enjoy a visit to Rochford for its picturesque Black Hills scenery. The **Moonshine Gulch Saloon** is also a popular lunch stop among fishermen, motorcyclists, ATV riders and those biking the nearby Mickelson Trail. Contact the saloon at (605) 584-2743.

91 COSMOS MYSTERY AREA

The laws of nature don't seem to apply at this mysterious area; balls roll uphill, and people on level ground appear to be standing on the wall or at impossible angles. In short, it's one of those places you just have to see to believe. Interactive tours of the unique mystery house take about 30 minutes and promise to entertain all ages, even teenagers!

Open April through October; Admission charged; 24040 Cosmos Rd. (17 miles south of Rapid City along US Hwy. 16), Rapid City, SD 57702; (605) 343-9802; www.cosmosmysteryarea.com

92 CHAPEL IN THE HILLS

Adorned with intricate woodcarvings, this church is a replica of the 850-year-old Stavkirke (Stave Church) in Norway. Surrounded by a serene park setting, the church is a popular place for summer weddings. There's also a Norwegian Log Cabin Museum and a grass-roofed log building that houses a gift shop. A Meditation Trail offers a leisurely path that winds into the hillside behind the chapel. Benches and statuary along the trail provide additional places for reflection, prayer or meditation. Vespers are held nightly at the church at 7:30 p.m. from Memorial Day through Labor Day.

Open May to October; Free admission; 3788 Chapel Ln. (W SD Hwy. 44), Rapid City, SD 57702; (605) 342-8281; www.chapel-in-the-hills.org

Intricate woodcarvings make this Stavkirke an interesting place to visit in Rapid City

93 BERLIN WALL EXHIBIT IN MEMORIAL PARK

Near Rapid Creek and the Rushmore Plaza Civic Center, this outdoor exhibit features two 12-foot segments of the Berlin Wall, accompanied by photographs and informational displays. In all, Memorial Park covers 27.5 acres, and it includes a band shell, a rose garden and memorials that pay tribute to the area's pioneers, veterans and the victims of Rapid City's infamous 1972 flood.

Open year-round; Free admission; 444 N Mount Rushmore Rd., Rapid City, SD 57701; (800) 487-3223; www.visitrapidcity.com/things-to-do/attractions/memorial-park-berlin-wall-exhibit

94 PETRIFIED FOREST OF THE BLACK HILLS

The geology of the Black Hills is showcased with a 15-minute film about the region's rocks and minerals, as well as museum displays and 25 acres of petrified forest to explore. The area includes the Gallery of Stone Rock Shop and is adjacent to a large RV park with camping, cabins and a heated pool.

Open April through October; Admission charged8220 Elk Creek Rd. (I-90 Exit 46), Piedmont, SD 57769; (605) 787-4560 or (800) 846-2267; www.elkcreekresort.net

NEAT TO KNOW:

One hundred miles east of Rapid City, off I-90 Exit 152, the Badlands Petrified Gardens at Kadoka include a large display of petrified trees and prehistoric fossils. Open mid-April through October; admission charged. For more information, call (605) 837-2448.

95 TERMESPHERE GALLERY

Art enthusiasts will marvel at the Termesphere Gallery, which features the work of artist Dick Termes, who paints on spheres. Nearly 30 termespheres rotate from ceiling motors in his sphere-shaped home gallery outside Spearfish. Termespheres can also be viewed at the Adams Museum in Deadwood (see page 52) and the Spearfish City Library.

Open year-round, Call for gallery hours; Free admission; 1920 Christensen Dr., Spearfish, SD 57783; (605) 642-4805; http://termespheres.com

NEAT TO KNOW:

In the heart of Spearfish is the quaint campus of **Black Hills State University**. Founded in 1883, it was the first college built in South Dakota and was originally named Dakota Normal School.

96 THOEN STONE MONUMENT

Though Lieutenant Colonel Custer and his expedition are credited with finding gold in the Black Hills in 1874, many believe that Ezra Kind and his party were the first to discover gold in the Black Hills in 1834, some forty years earlier. However, the seven men, who were trespassing on American Indian land, were killed by American Indians before they could return home. But, before his death, Kind etched their story on a stone, which was discovered at the base of Spearfish's Lookout Mountain in 1887 by Louis Thoen. The original stone, named in Thoen's honor, is on display in the Adams Museum in Deadwood (see page 52). To view a replica that denotes the original location of the stone, a short hiking path can be accessed near the former Passion Play amphitheater parking lot. For more information, contact the Spearfish Chamber of Commerce.

Accessible year-round, weather permitting; (605) 642-2626; Spearfish, SD; www.blackhillsthehike.com/thoen-stone/

97 GEOGRAPHIC CENTER OF THE UNITED STATES

In 1959, Belle Fourche was given special acclaim as "Center of the Nation" by the U.S. Coast and Geodetic Survey, after Alaska and Hawaii were admitted to the Union that same year. Formerly, when only America's 48 states were considered, the center of the nation was deemed to be at Smith Center, Kansas. A historic marker denoted Belle Fourche's "Center of the Nation" designation for decades, but in 2007, a 21-foot-diameter monument made of etched South Dakota granite with a 12-inch bronze marker from the National Geodetic Survey was placed near the Tri-State Museum in Belle Fourche to create more awareness for the unique claim to fame. An Avenue of Flags with each of the fifty state flags adorns the short path that leads to the monument. Visitors can enjoy the park-like setting, as well as the pioneer and cowboy exhibits of the Tri-State Museum. An authentic log cabin and sheep wagon are on display outside the building and are fun for younger children to peer into.

The actual marker is 20 miles north of Belle Fourche; it's located at latitude 44°58'N and longitude 103°46'W. Follow US Hwy. 85 north from Belle Fourche for 13 miles. Turn west on Harding Road (also known as Old Hwy. 85) and drive 7.8 miles.

Accessible year-round; Free admission; 415 5th Ave., Belle Fourche, SD 57717; (605) 723-1200; www.thetristatemuseum.com/

NEAT TO KNOW:

Bentonite, which is mined near Belle Fourche, can be found in everyday products such as crayons, glue, paint, shoe polish and spark plugs.

The historical marker at the geographic center of the United States

Entertainment abounds in the Black Hills, and much of it is set to music. From Old West settings to Broadway-style shows, there's something for every taste. So kick up your heels and treat the family to a night out and a special show. Your outing just might become a family tradition each time you visit the Black Hills.

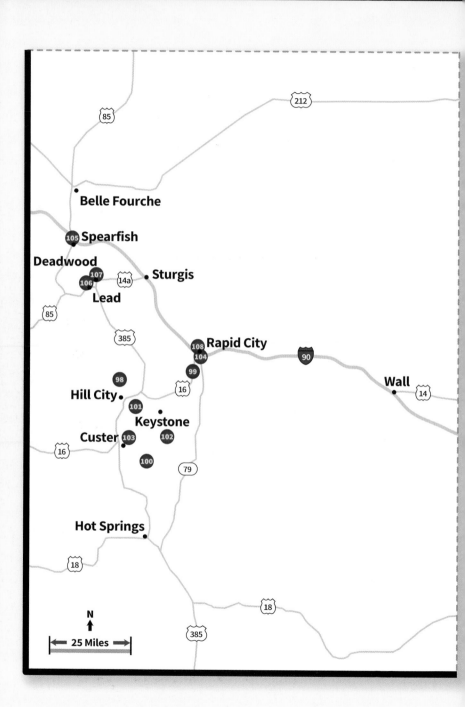

Western Style

Summer Sensations

Year-Round Curtain Calls

Western Style

If it is a chuckwagon dinner and a Western music show you hunger for, there are several options during the summer months throughout the Black Hills.

98 CIRCLE B CHUCKWAGON SUPPER AND COWBOY MUSIC SHOW

Set amid the forest of the Black Hills and adjacent to the High Country Guest Ranch, which includes cabin and camping accommodations, the Circle B Chuckwagon includes the storefront of a Western town, gem panning, an on-site wood-carver, mock gunfights, wax bullet pistol shooting and a gift shop, making it enjoyable for all ages. The venue opens at 4 p.m. daily and the dinner bell rings at 5:30 p.m. Dinner is served rain or shine in the chuckwagon barn and features baked beans, a foil-wrapped potato, BBQ beef or chicken, applesauce, biscuits and spice cake. After dinner, guests are entertained with an authentic cowboy music show, along with a side dish of ranch humor. For guests looking for more than just an evening of entertainment, **High Country Guest Ranch** also offers cabin rentals, trail rides, ATV rentals and other amenities.

Open Monday through Saturday, Memorial Day through Labor Day; Fee charged; 12138 Ray Smith Dr. (at High Country Guest Ranch), Hill City, SD 57745; (605) 574-2129; www.circle-b-ranch.com; http://highcountryranch.com

99 FORT HAYS CHUCKWAGON SUPPER AND OLD WEST TOWN DINNER SHOW

"Eatin', fiddlin', strummin' and drummin' till the cows come home" is the tagline used at the Fort Hays Chuckwagon and Dinner Show. Conveniently located five miles south of Rapid City on US Hwy. 16 on the way to Mount Rushmore, the Fort Hays setting features an old West town. Guests can explore original buildings from the *Dances With Wolves* movie set, which was filmed in South Dakota. An outdoor wooden boardwalk leads visitors from one building to the next, and craftsmen are on hand daily to share their skills from 7:30 a.m. to 6:30 p.m. Workshop areas include a tin shop, a rope shop, a post office, a blacksmith shop, a sawmill and a penny press. At 6:30 p.m. it's time for supper, with meals served on tin plates made on the premises in the tin shop. (You can make or buy one of your own on site, too.) Baked beans, chuckwagon potatoes, sliced beef or baked chicken, ranch biscuits, applesauce and spice cake round out the menu. At 7:15 p.m. the Fort Hays Wranglers take the stage with a music and variety show that delivers toe-tapping fun.

Additionally, Fort Hays serves all-you-can-eat cowboy pancakes each morning until 11 a.m., and offers a day-long chartered bus tour of the Black Hills that begins with the breakfast and ends with the chuckwagon supper and music show.

Open seven days a week, mid-May thru early October; Fee charged; 2255 Fort Hayes Dr. (5 miles south of Rapid City on US Hwy. 16), Rapid City, SD 57702; (888) 342-3113; http://mountrushmoretours.com/

100 BLUE BELL LODGE HAYRIDE AND CHUCK WAGON COOKOUT

You'll hop aboard a hayride for this evening outing. Guests are treated to a souvenir hat and bandanna and serenaded with cowboy songs as the old-time wagon makes its way to a meadow in Custer State Park to enjoy an evening feast. The ride is about 45 minutes, and buffalo and other wildlife are usually spotted during the journey. Once in the meadow, a hearty meal of grilled steaks, cowboy beans, cornbread and honey, potato salad, coleslaw, watermelon and cookies awaits. More music follows the meal to round out the memorable evening. Hayrides depart at 5 p.m. nightly from Blue Bell Lodge and return by 8 p.m. For reservations call (605) 255-4531 or (888) 875-0001. For more about Custer State Park, see page 67.

The Blue Bell Lodge Hayride and its chuckwagon cookout

Cookout offered Memorial Day to early October; Fee charged; Custer State Park (605) 255-4515; http://custerresorts.com/activities/activities-in-the-park/hayride-chuck-wagon-cookout/

101 CHUCK WAGON DINNER SHOW AT PALMER GULCH

This open-air chuckwagon dinner-and-music show takes place in a remote mountain meadow surrounded by the Black Hills National Forest. Guests can chose to saddle a horse and take a trail ride to the show or ride in a horse-drawn covered wagon. Steaks grilled over an open fire and Dutch-oven side dishes make for an authentic cowboy meal. Then, enjoy a peach or pear cobbler dessert while listening to the sweet crooning of cowboy music.

Available mid-June through mid-August; Fee charged; 12620 SD Hwy. 244 (between Keystone and Hill City), Hill City, SD 57745; (605) 574-3412; http://ridesouthdakota.com/rushmore-horseback-riding/chuck-wagon-dinner-show/

Trail ride to the Chuch Wagon Dinner Show

NEAT TO KNOW:

The Comedy Western Gun Show is presented three times daily at the Red Garter Saloon on Keystone's Main Street. The rustic cowboy actors look tough, but it's just an act—this is a family show. Presented Memorial Day through mid-September at 1:30, 3:30 and 5:30 p.m.; no shows on Sundays; admission charged. Call (605) 666-4274 or visit http://redgartersaloon.com to learn more.

Summer Sensations

Broadway performances in the Black Hills? Yes, it's true. These venues garner great acclaim throughout the region.

102 BLACK HILLS PLAYHOUSE

In 1946, the first Black Hills Playhouse performance was given in the tranquility of Custer State Park, and the live theater productions have thrilled audiences ever since. Four Broadway-quality shows are presented through the summer season in this one-of-a-kind setting located amid a quiet solitude of pine trees within the state park. *Shrek The Musical, Godspell, Grease* and *The Secret Garden* are among some of the past productions brought to the Black Hills Playhouse stage. A small concession stand and gift shop caters to theatergoers before the show and during intermission.

Performances presented Tuesday through Saturday at 7:30 p.m. and Wednesday and Sunday at 2 p.m., June through August; Admission charged; Custer State Park, 24834 Playhouse Rd., Custer, SD 57730; (605) 255-4141 or (605) 255-4910; www.blackhillsplayhouse.com

Enjoy live theater in the Black Hills

103 THE GRAND MAGIC SHOW

One amazing illusion after the next is what attendees can expect at The Grand Magic Show, which features internationally awarded performer Duane Laflin, who has performed around the world including regular-run shows in Pigeon Forge, TN, and Branson, MO. Each 90-minute show includes a fast-paced series of mind-boggling illusions—many of which rival big city entertainers. Laflin also entertains with a dose of comedy and several opportunities for audience participation. Performances are presented in the Buffalo Ridge Theatre, a spacious facility with seating for 500.

On Sundays throughout the summer, instead of magic, it's music that takes the stage, featuring the Grand Jamboree. Laflin is joined by a variety of local, professional musicians performing songs from the '50s, Elvis, old-time country, modern country, gospel tunes and more. The 2-hour show concludes with a heart-touching patriotic tribute.

Performances presented Memorial Day through Labor Day; Admission charged; 370 W Mount Rushmore Rd., Custer, SD 57730; (406) 291-2004; www.grandmagicshow.com

Year-Round Curtain Calls

Community theater and musical productions are presented at the following locations throughout the year. Although most are intended for adult audiences, some offer special productions geared for children during their season. Call or check their websites for a list of upcoming performances.

104 BLACK HILLS COMMUNITY THEATRE

The Black Hills Community Theatre (BHCT) has operated in various locations throughout Rapid City for five decades, and in 2012 settled into its permanent home in the Performing Arts Center of Rapid City. BHCT's season includes five main stage productions, a dinner theater fundraiser, and shows by the Cherry Street Players (BHCT's children's troupe) and the Well Done Players (BHCT's troupe of well-seasoned actors). A number of other special events, including national and regional performers, are regularly featured at the Performing Arts Center. Black Hills Community Theatre also operates a Costume Shop, which is open to the public for costume rentals throughout the year.

601 Columbus St., PO Box 4007, Rapid City, SD 57701; (605) 394-1787; http://bhct.org/

105 MATTHEWS OPERA HOUSE & ARTS CENTER

Opened in 1906, the Matthews Opera House hosted stage productions and traveling shows through the 1930s. As movie theaters came into vogue, the opera house was less frequently used for live theater events and instead became a practice basketball court, a shooting gallery and occasional dance hall. The facility eventually began to deteriorate, and by the mid-1980s a restoration effort was pursued by Spearfish citizens; full restoration was completed in 2006, marking the centennial year of the Matthews Opera House. Today, the venue hosts an ongoing array of live theater, concerts and art events throughout the year. The Spearfish Arts Center is operated in conjunction with the facility and features a gallery displaying the work of local artists.

612 N Main St., Spearfish, SD 57783; (605) 642-7973; www.matthewsopera.com

106 HISTORIC HOMESTAKE OPERA HOUSE

Completed in August 1914, the Homestake Opera House was built with stunning craftsmanship and was soon known as the "Jewel of the Black Hills." In addition to providing a venue for quality theater, it housed a recreation building that included a bowling alley, pool hall and swimming pool. Having endured a devastating fire in 1984, today the opera house is undergoing massive reconstruction to restore the 1000-seat theater. Performances are held intermittently throughout the year, and tours are offered September through April by appointment for a nominal fee.

313 W Main St., PO Box 412, Lead, SD 57754; (605) 584-2067; www.leadoperahouse.org/

107 DEADWOOD MOUNTAIN GRAND EVENTS CENTER

In 2011, an extensive renovation to the former Homestake Slime Plant in Deadwood was completed, creating a hotel, casino, restaurant and entertainment venue. The spacious facility now brings a steady stream of nationally acclaimed talent to the Black Hills year-round, featuring acts like Foreigner, Huey Lewis and the News, Dwight Yoakam and Dolly Parton.

1906 Deadwood Mountain Dr., PO Box 308, Deadwood, SD 57732; (605) 559-0386 or (877) 907-GRAND; www.deadwoodmountaingrand.com/

108 RUSHMORE PLAZA CIVIC CENTER

Broadway musicals, Las Vegas comedians and a variety of musical performers are regularly featured at the Rushmore Plaza Civic Center's fine arts theater.

444 N Mount Rushmore Rd., Rapid City, SD 57701; (605) 394-4115 or (800) GOT-MINE; https://gotmine.com/events/box-office

NEAT TO KNOW: TWO UNIQUE THEATRES

Theater buffs will likely enjoy watching the big screen at two notable Black Hills theaters. The **Historic Elks Theatre** at 512 6th Street in downtown Rapid City dates back to the early 1900s. The building opened in 1912 as an Elks Lodge and opera house, and in 1929 movies began to be shown in the theatre. Ownership changed hands over the years, and it was even closed for a period, but today, the Elks is a cherished part of Rapid City's history. Much of the original ornate architecture within the building remains, and the main theatre features a balcony and impressively large screen. Two smaller screening rooms have been added to the facility. Second-run movies at a discounted rate are typically featured. The theater is open year-round. Call (605) 343-7888 or visit www.elkstheatre.com.

Twenty minutes south of Rapid City along SD Hwy. 79 at Hermosa is **Roy's Black Hills Twin Drive-In Theatre**. Moviegoers can experience the nostalgia of yester-year by watching a film from their vehicle and listening to the audio through their radio. Many patrons bring lawn chairs and perch in the back end of their pickup. As the name suggests, there are two screens—dubbed the east and west screens. They are each 80 feet wide, and all-digital for sharp images. Roy's has the distinction of being the first "all-digital drive-in theatre" in the country. Concessions and a children's playground are on site. Movies begin at dark and are shown mid-May through September. Call (605) 255-5333 or visit www.facebook.com/roysblackhillstwindrivein.

FOR OTHER ENTERTAINING PERFORMANCES, SEE ALSO:

Evening Lighting Ceremony, Mount Rushmore, Keystone, page 12; Laser Light Show, Crazy Horse, Custer, page 18; Gunslingers reenactment and Trial of Jack McCall, Deadwood, page 20; Storybook Island Children's Theatre, Rapid City, page 93

Index

View from Black Elk Peak

Index by City

Note: All cities are in South Dakota unless otherwise noted.

DEADWOOD/LEAD (www.deadwood.org and www.lead.sd.us)

ROCHFORD

About the Author

Kindra Gordon first began spinning stories when she was in second grade and still enjoys the thrill of putting words to paper. Raised on a ranch in South Dakota, she is an agricultural journalism graduate from South Dakota State University in Brookings. Today, she works as a freelance writer for national cattle magazines including *BEEF*, *Angus Journal* and *Western Cowman*. She has also written travel articles for AAA's *Home&Away* magazine and has taught newspaper design and feature writing as an adjunct professor in the Mass Communications Department at Black Hills State University in Spearfish, South Dakota.

Kindra and her husband Bruce live near Sturgis, South Dakota with their four children, and they wake up everyday to an inspiring view of the Black Hills.